Understand Your Diesel Engine
and Save Money
First Editon

Robert L. Lekse

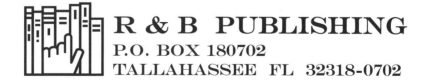

R & B PUBLISHING
P.O. BOX 180702
TALLAHASSEE FL 32318-0702

Understand Your Diesel Engine and Save Money. First edition.
Copyright © 2002 by Robert L. Lekse.

Heartfelt thanks to Rosanna, Barb, and Tarik. I couldn't have done it without you.

Editing:
Rosanna Gervasi
Tarik Noriega

Illustrations:
Barbara Solomon

Library of Congress Control Number: 2002093102

ISBN No. 0-9722695-0-9 Softbound

This book is dedicated to the memory of my parents, Frank and Mildred Lekse.

Contents

Introduction

I have worked in the obscure diesel fuel injection industry for 20 years as a diesel fuel injection technician. My job has been to rebuild, recondition, and remanufacture diesel fuel injection components, mainly injection pumps and injectors. These components are the heart of the diesel engine. Understanding the basic functions of these components and how they interact to power an engine is an ongoing challenge. The industry is very diverse with dozens of pump and injector types, and thousands of variations. New models and variations are continually being designed and manufactured.

Troubleshooting and solving diesel engine problems has been another facet of this work. Understanding the basic concepts and years of applying them to solve engine running (runability) problems has enabled me to sift through and sort all this information into a model of what makes a diesel engine work, and what to look for when an engine doesn't work correctly.

For years I have seen a lack of basic and easily understandable information available for diesel engine owners, and the same costly mistakes made. Many misconceptions exist about the operation of a diesel engine. Misconceptions lead to misdiagnosis, and that can cost you money. The objectives of this handbook are to describe the basic operations of the diesel engine and fuel system and to give a clear understanding about the common causes and symptoms of many diesel engine and fuel system problems.

This handbook applies to all five diesel applications; agricultural, industrial, marine, trucking, and automotive. No matter what the engine is in, it is still a diesel.

The content of this book is structured to present general information and theory first. Once you understand how and why things work, we can go from general information to more specific information.

This handbook is written for diesel engine owners who want to understand their engines and avoid costly mistakes. *Whether or not you work on your own engine*, this handbook will help you identify symptoms and probable causes of any runability problem. "Understand Your Diesel Engine and Save Money" will also help you maximize the reliability and extend the life of your diesel engine. Diesel mechanics will benefit from the information in this book, as well.

The illustrations and descriptions of the diesel engines and fuel injection systems are generalized and simplified in order to focus on important basic concepts. I have included helpful tips for particular fuel injection systems, but it is beyond the scope of this book to present excessively technical details of particular engines or fuel injection systems. Every engine and fuel system type has its own peculiarities. I will describe the basic functions of diesel engines and fuel injection systems and how to interpret the symptoms of a malfunctioning engine.

In writing this handbook, my goals are: 1) to present information that gives the diesel engine owner or mechanic greater knowledge to troubleshoot and solve many engine and fuel system problems as quickly and as cost effectively as possible; 2) to present an outline of proper maintenance since a significant number of failures are caused by a lack of maintenance; and 3) to present other related information that helps to save you money.

Keeping your diesel engine maintained and running efficiently maximizes your fuel economy, extends the life of your engine, and minimizes the formation of pollutants. Cleaner running diesel engines contribute much less to air pollution. With millions of diesel engines in service worldwide, better engine maintenance, adjustments, and repairs can only improve the quality of the air we breathe.

Safety

I cannot stress enough the need for conscientious safety habits. I will point out potential safety concerns throughout this handbook. Before working on an engine, I recommend reading the safety section of your equipment or service manual.

Quite often one must work on or around an engine that is running or cranking at starting speed. You must be aware of any part of your body, loose clothing, cords, tools, rags, etc., which could come into contact with any hot or moving parts. If you let an engine run without the intake manifold or air filter installed, be aware of the tremendous vacuum that the engine creates. An engine running with an open intake manifold can suck in anything close to it, including your hands.

When priming or bleeding a fuel system, keep in mind that while diesel fuel is not flammable like gasoline, it is combustible. Diesel fuel can ignite with sufficient heat, such as from a hot exhaust manifold. Wearing safety glasses should be mandatory when working on an engine.

Diesel engines are used in a variety of applications. Please be aware of all safety concerns for your equipment and use common sense. This book addresses safety issues relating only to engines and fuel systems, not to specific applications.

Chapter 1 - How Does the Diesel Engine Work?

Before the turn of the 20th Century, an industrial engineer named Rudolf Diesel developed one of the first engines that operated on the principle of compression ignition. Several years later, Robert Bosch designed and manufactured a practical fuel system for the diesel engine. Although designs and capabilities have grown and changed enormously, we can understand today's diesel engine as easily as we can understand the first diesel engines from more than a century ago.

This handbook emphasizes the function of the fuel injection system more than the function of the engine. All diesel engine models have their own peculiarities, but basically, an engine is an engine. Each engine cylinder acts as an air compressor. On the other hand, diesel fuel injection systems come in a wide variety of models and variations. Although any diesel fuel injection system must accomplish the same tasks, the types and varieties of injection pumps and injectors are numerous.

Compression loss due to engine cylinder wear, valve leakage, or incorrect valve timing may affect engine runability depending on the severity of compression loss. Unless stated otherwise, all engine examples in this book assume that the engine is in good working order.

To understand the basic concept of the diesel, let's first compare the diesel engine to the gasoline (Otto) engine. For the sake of comparison, a four-stroke gasoline engine with a carburetor will be used. Two-stroke engines will be discussed later.

In a gasoline or diesel engine cylinder there is a piston with rings that move up and down on a connecting rod, which is being moved by a rotating crankshaft. On top of the cylinder is a head that contains an intake valve and an exhaust valve, which is being operated by a camshaft to open and close these valves at the correct times. The sequences of operation for four-stroke gasoline and diesel engines are:

Four-stroke gasoline cycle

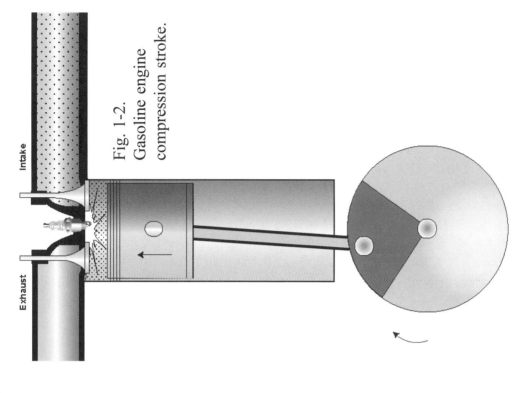

Fig. 1-1.
Gasoline engine
intake stroke.

1 Spark plug
2 Exhaust valve
3 Intake valve
4 Piston
5 Cylinder
6 Connecting rod
7 Crankshaft

Fig. 1-2.
Gasoline engine
compression stroke.

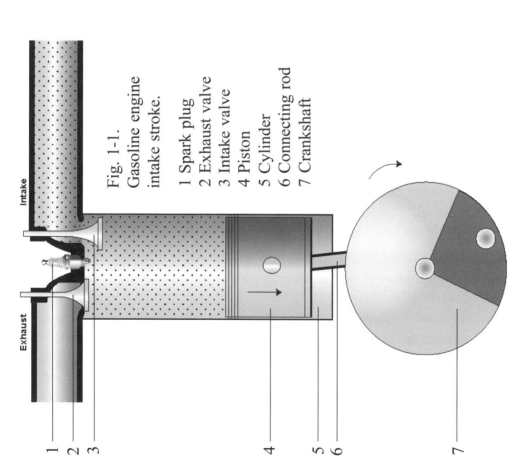

Intake: The piston moves down with the intake valve open and draws in a carburized air/fuel mixture. At the bottom of the stroke the intake valve closes.

Compression: The piston moves up to compress the air/fuel mixture. Near the top of the stroke, the spark plug fires, igniting the air/fuel mixture.

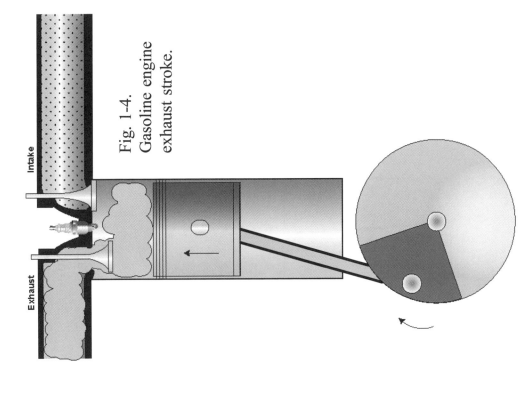

Fig. 1-4.
Gasoline engine exhaust stroke.

Exhaust: The exhaust valve opens and the piston moves up to push the exhaust gases out of the cylinder.

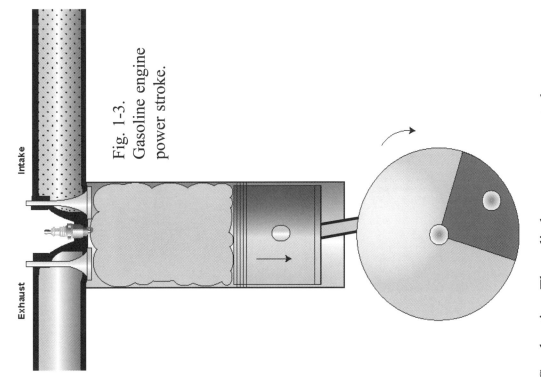

Fig. 1-3.
Gasoline engine power stroke.

Combustion: The cylinder pressure created by the expansion and explosion of the hot compressed air/fuel mixture forces the piston down. This is the power stroke.

Four-stroke diesel cycle

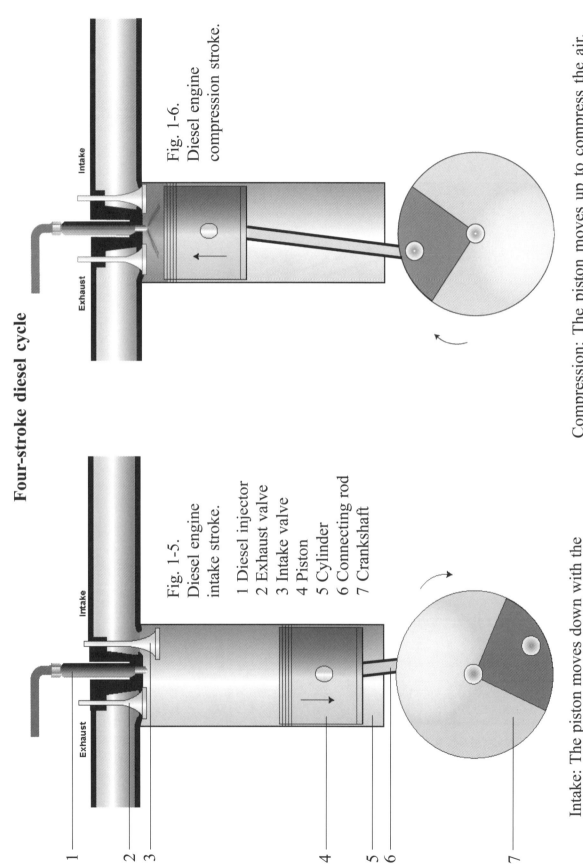

Fig. 1-6.
Diesel engine
compression stroke.

Fig. 1-5.
Diesel engine
intake stroke.

1 Diesel injector
2 Exhaust valve
3 Intake valve
4 Piston
5 Cylinder
6 Connecting rod
7 Crankshaft

Intake

Exhaust

Compression: The piston moves up to compress the air. Compressing air creates heat. Near the top of the stroke, the fuel system injects an atomized amount of fuel that expands and burns when it contacts the hot compressed air.

Intake: The piston moves down with the intake valve open and draws in only air. The intake valve closes at the bottom of the stroke.

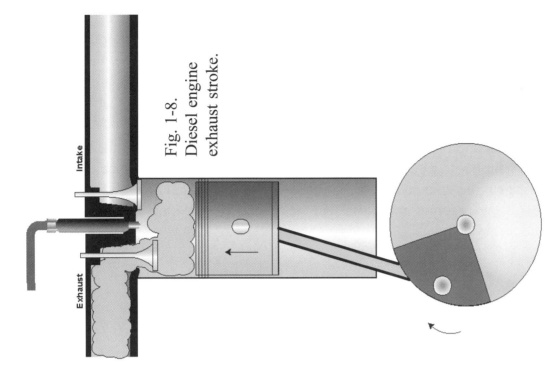

Fig. 1-8. Diesel engine exhaust stroke.

Exhaust: The exhaust valve opens and the piston moves up to push the exhaust gases out of the cylinder.

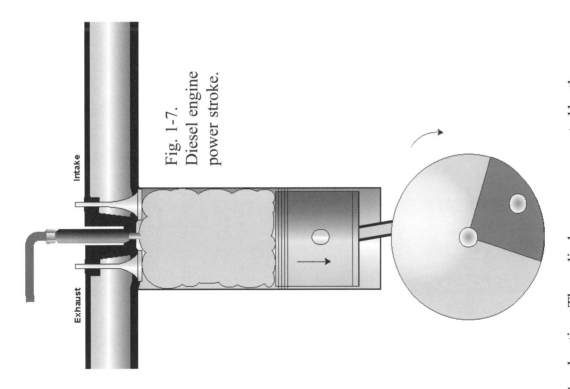

Fig. 1-7. Diesel engine power stroke.

Combustion: The cylinder pressure created by the expansion and explosion of the atomized fuel and the hot compressed air forces the piston down. This is the power stroke.

Atomized fuel from a diesel injector is similar to spray from an aerosol can, but at much higher pressure. A diesel engine can create the heat needed to ignite the atomized fuel because a diesel engine has a much higher compression ratio than a gasoline engine -- from 15 to 1 up to 25 to 1. Compressing air quickly to approximately 5% of its original volume creates a tremendous amount of heat. Atomized diesel fuel needs about 600° F to burn correctly.

This is the basic concept of a four-stroke diesel engine. As you can see, the moving engine parts are very similar to a gasoline engine. A diesel engine usually has heavier duty parts than a gasoline engine to create higher compression and withstand extra stress. The four-stroke cycles of the gasoline and diesel engines are also very similar. The biggest difference is in the fuel system.

Chapter 2 - The Diesel Fuel Injection System

The diesel fuel injection system is the heart of the diesel engine. While gasoline and diesel engines are very similar, gasoline and diesel fuel systems are very different.

The diesel fuel injection industry has provided us with numerous pump and injector designs and variations. The injection pump with injection line and injector is the most common system in use today. The following descriptions are of injection pump/injection line/injector systems. Other fuel system designs are discussed in Chapter 8.

Injection pumps in the pump/line/injector systems can be divided into two basic categories, distributor injection pumps and inline injection pumps. Distributor injection pumps, commonly called rotary pumps, have the injection outlets in a circular formation like a distributor for a gasoline engine. Inline injection pumps have the injection outlets in a straight line. Some inline pumps have two rows of injection outlets. Distributor pumps have one pumping unit called a hydraulic 'head and rotor,' which provides fuel to *all* engine cylinders. Inline pumps have one pumping unit called the plunger and barrel (P&B), which provides fuel to *each* cylinder. An inline injection pump on a six-cylinder diesel engine has six P&Bs.

For a four-stroke diesel engine, the injection pump turns at half-engine speed, like a distributor in a four-stroke gasoline engine. In the time it takes a four-stroke engine to make two complete revolutions, the injection pump makes one complete revolution. The fuel injection system only needs to inject fuel while the engine is on the compression stroke.

Keep in mind that most people who work on diesel engines never work on the fuel injection systems except to remove and/or install them. It takes special tools, equipment, and training to analyze and service fuel injection components properly. Occasionally, a minor repair can be made on a fuel injection unit without removing it from the engine. Only after eliminating all other possible causes of an engine runability problem should a fuel injection unit be removed for testing, repair, or replacement. I recommend that a factory authorized fuel injection shop handle your fuel system repairs. Remanufactured or new units are also available for exchange at diesel fuel injection shops or equipment dealers.

Inline injection pump

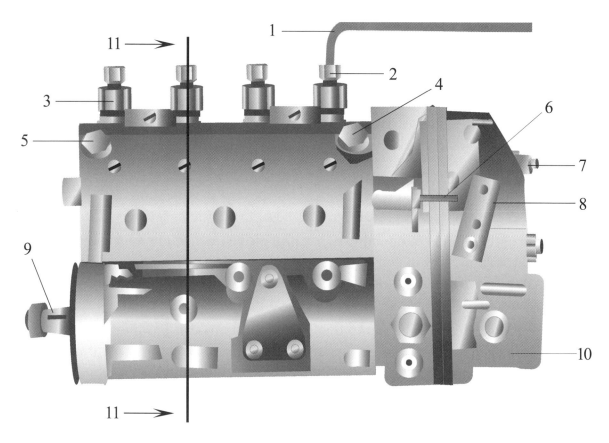

Fig. 2-1. Inline injection pump.

1 Injection line	6 High-speed screw	11 Cut-away view for Fig. 2-2
2 Injection line nut	7 Idle screw	
3 Injection outlet fitting	8 Throttle lever	
4 Fuel inlet screw	9 Drive shaft (camshaft)	
5 Overflow valve (screw)	10 Governor housing	

Fig. 2-1 illustrates a typical Robert Bosch inline injection pump. A drive gear or drive adapter attached to the injection pump drive shaft is driven by the engine.

Any diesel fuel injection pump and injector must accomplish the same three tasks. It must pressurize the fuel; it must time the delivery of fuel into the cylinder's hot compressed air; and it must meter, or measure, the amount of fuel being delivered.

Figure 2-2 shows a cut-away view of an inline injection pump as it pressurizes, times, and meters fuel for injection. The inlet screw and overflow screw are shown on opposite sides of the injection pump housing and the injection pump is pictured larger than the engine cylinder to show details.

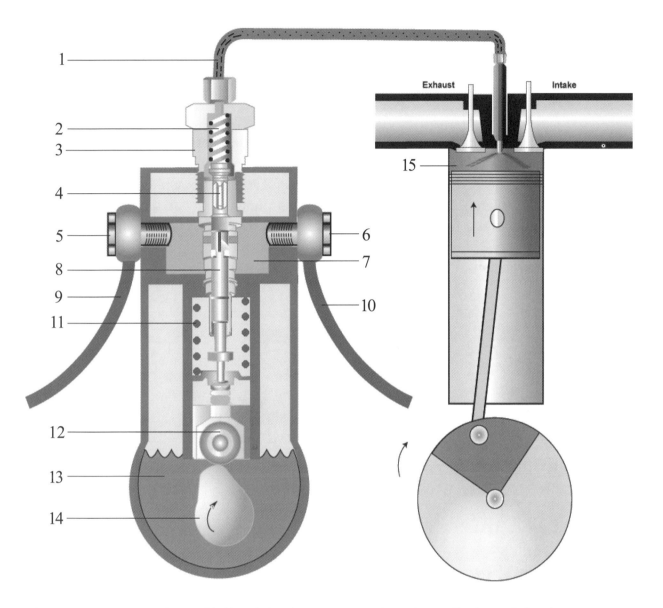

Fig. 2.2. Cut-away view of inline injection pump and engine cylinder at injection.

1 Injection line (steel tubing)
2 Delivery valve spring
3 Injection outlet fitting
4 Delivery valve
5 Inlet screw (flow through)

6 Overflow screw (restrictor)
7 Fuel gallery
8 Plunger and barrel (P&B)
9 Inlet fuel line from final
  stage fuel filter

10 Return fuel line
11 Plunger return spring
12 Roller tappet
13 Lube oil
14 Camshaft lobe
15 Combustion chamber

    After the intake stroke, the engine piston moves up to compress air and create heat. Near the top of the compression stroke, the injection pump and injector create a pressurized, timed, and metered burst of fuel. The fuel pressure created by the injection pump opens the injector, which atomizes and distributes the fuel into the engine cylinder's hot compressed air. The atomized fuel expands and explodes, creating cylinder pressure that forces the piston down for the power stroke.

The three tasks of a fuel injection pump are pressurizing, timing, and metering. Let's take a closer look at each task.

Pressurizing

Diesel fuel injection systems pressurize fuel by a process of high-speed hydraulic pumping. The pressures currently being developed by these pumping parts range from about 2000 pounds per square inch (psi) up to 25,000 psi. The basic pumping unit designed by Robert Bosch is still in use today; a cylindrical pump plunger fitted to a matching casing or barrel. The plungers and barrels are fitted as closely as fifty millionths of an inch, but they slide freely and very fast to pump the fuel. The oiliness, or lubricity, of the diesel fuel is the P&B's only lubrication.

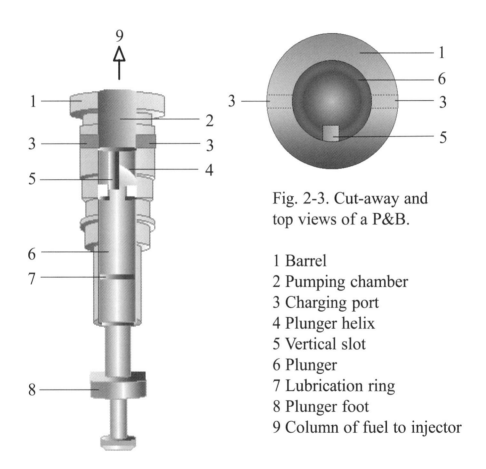

Fig. 2-3. Cut-away and top views of a P&B.

1 Barrel
2 Pumping chamber
3 Charging port
4 Plunger helix
5 Vertical slot
6 Plunger
7 Lubrication ring
8 Plunger foot
9 Column of fuel to injector

The P&B creates pressure by pushing against a column of fuel in the injection line which pushes against the injector connected to the other end of the injection line. When the injection line pressure reaches the preset opening pressure of the injector, from 1500 psi to 5000 psi, the injector needle valve opens and delivers an atomized amount of fuel into the combustion chamber.

The sequence of operation for a P&B is:

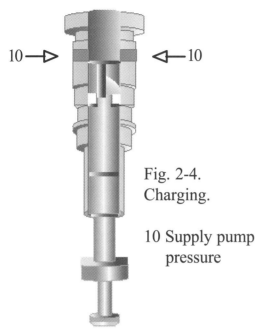

Fig. 2-4.
Charging.

10 Supply pump
pressure

Diesel fuel under supply pump pressure charges (fills) the pumping chamber.

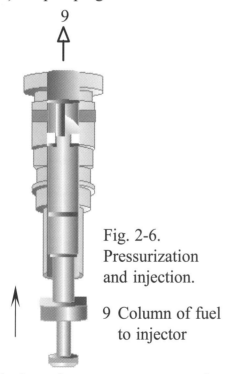

Fig. 2-6.
Pressurization
and injection.

9 Column of fuel
to injector

After port closing, plunger movement pushes the column of fuel in the injection line towards the injector. Injection pressure is created quickly and the injector nozzle opens and delivers an atomized burst of fuel into the engine cylinder.

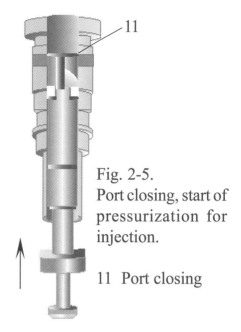

Fig. 2-5.
Port closing, start of pressurization for injection.

11 Port closing

The top edge of the plunger closes the charging ports. At this point, the column of fuel between the pumping chamber and the injector is sealed.

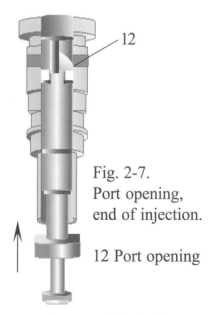

Fig. 2-7.
Port opening, end of injection.

12 Port opening

Injection continues until the helix uncovers the bottom edge of the charge port. The pressure in the pumping chamber and injection line is relieved through the vertical slot. The injector needle valve snaps shut and injection ends quickly.

Timing

In a pump/line/injector system with an inline injection pump, each engine cylinder has its own corresponding pumping unit, injection line, and injector, as in Fig. 2-2, p. 11. Each pumping unit has its own camshaft lobe which rotates with the camshaft and causes the P&B to create injection pressure at the correct time for its corresponding cylinder. In an inline pump, the firing order is determined by the injection pump camshaft.

A common firing order for a four-cylinder engine is 1-3-4-2. When the piston in engine cylinder number one is near the top of the compression stroke, injection pump outlet number one creates injection pressure and the injector delivers fuel into the engine cylinder's hot compressed air. The piston in engine cylinder number three moves up next on the compression stroke. When the piston in engine cylinder number three is near the top of the compression stroke, injection pump outlet number three creates injection pressure and the injector delivers fuel into the cylinder's hot compressed air. The process continues for engine cylinder number four, then number two, then back to number one.

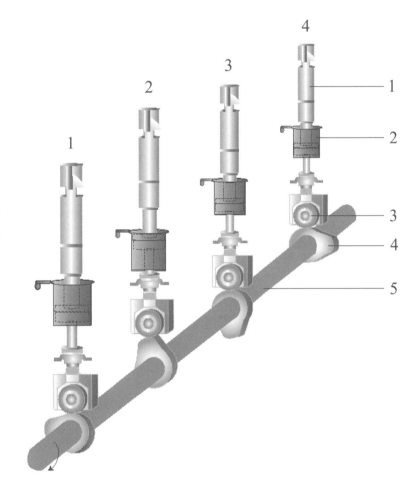

Fig. 2-8.
Plungers from a four-cylinder inline injection pump with number two plunger moving up to create injection pressure for engine cylinder number two.

1 Plunger
2 Control sleeve
3 Roller tappet
4 Camshaft lobe
5 Camshaft

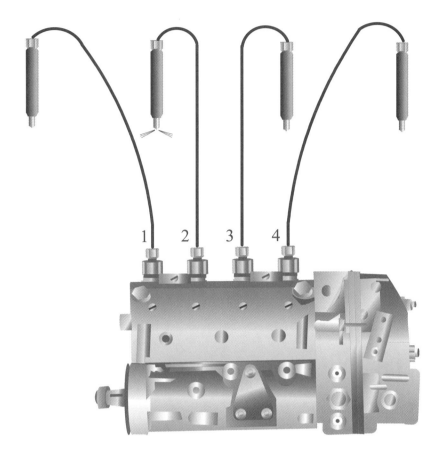

Fig. 2-9. Four-cylinder injection pump delivering fuel for engine cylinder number two (see Fig. 2-2, p. 11).

Injection timing is critical to make a diesel engine run correctly. Any diesel fuel injection system is timed to the engine by its relationship to the engine crankshaft. Each type of fuel injection system has a specific procedure to set injection timing or static timing. Figures 2-11 through 2-16 show six crankshaft angles and the corresponding piston positions. The movements of the crankshaft and piston are measured in crankshaft degrees. A crankshaft turning one full revolution, or 360 degrees, moves a piston up and down once.

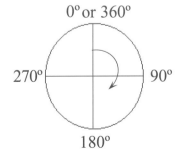

Fig. 2-10.

Degree values for points on a circle starting at 0° and moving clockwise.

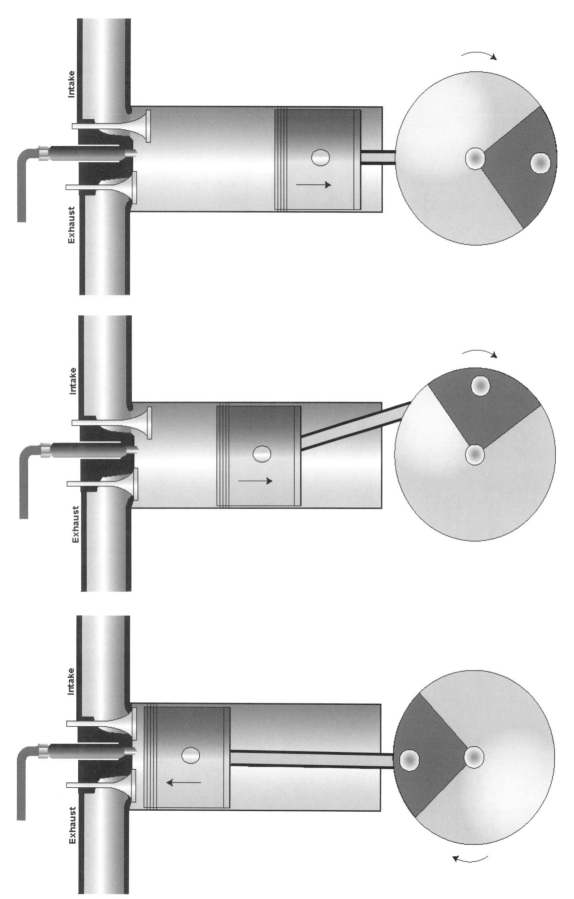

Fig. 2-13. Crankshaft angle 180°. Piston at 180° ATDC, 180° BTDC or bottom-dead-center (BDC).

Fig. 2-12. Crankshaft angle 90°. Piston at 90° after top-dead-center (ATDC), 270° before top-dead-center (BTDC).

Fig. 2-11. Crankshaft angle 0°. Piston at top-dead-center (TDC).

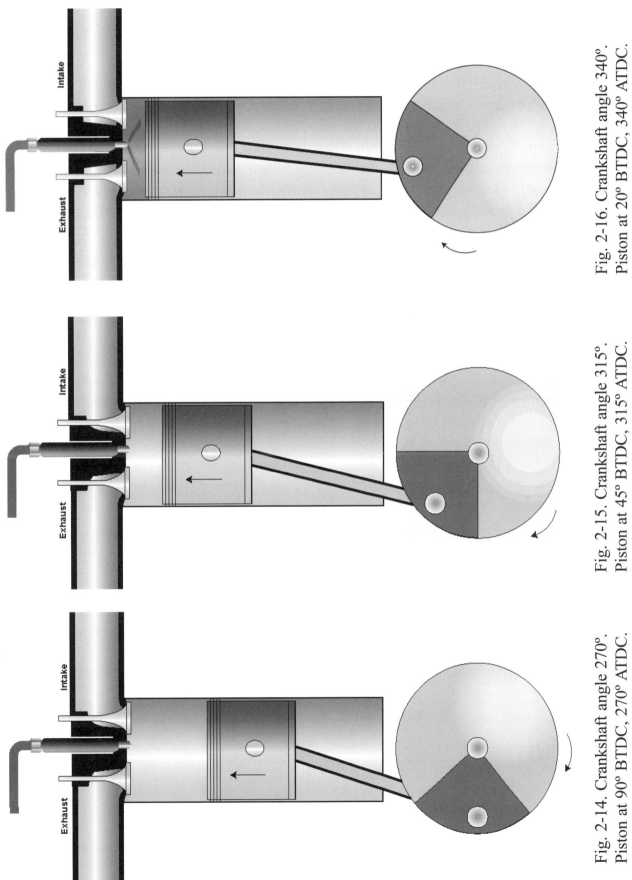

Fig. 2-16. Crankshaft angle 340°.
Piston at 20° BTDC, 340° ATDC.

Fig. 2-15. Crankshaft angle 315°.
Piston at 45° BTDC, 315° ATDC.

Fig. 2-14. Crankshaft angle 270°.
Piston at 90° BTDC, 270° ATDC.

The fuel must be injected just before TDC on the compression stroke. Depending on the engine, delivery will occur for each cylinder between 10° BTDC and 40° BTDC on the compression stroke. Figure 2-16, page 17, shows injection at 20° BTDC.

The objectives are to inject the fuel at the right time into the engine cylinder's hot compressed air; to create expanding gases which generate power by forcing the piston downwards; and to burn all of the fuel as completely as possible. An injection pump may have one or more timing devices to advance (happen sooner) or retard (happen later) the timing of injection for certain factors. Injection pumps and timing devices are engineered and adjusted (calibrated) to change the timing of injection for engine speed, load, and other conditions. For any working moment, the fuel injection system injects the fuel at the right time to burn all the fuel as completely as possible and make the maximum cylinder pressure occur just after TDC, which creates optimum power.

Figure 2-17 shows the relationship between cylinder pressure and crankshaft angle for a diesel engine cylinder on the compression and power strokes. At the time of injection, the piston has already made some compression and enough heat for expansion and combustion to occur. In this example, injection begins at 20° BTDC and ends at 15° BTDC. Typically, duration of injection will be 4-6 crankshaft degrees. After injection, expansion and combustion occur to dramatically increase cylinder pressure. Note that maximum cylinder pressure occurs just a few degrees ATDC. The cylinder pressure generated from expansion and combustion forces the piston down for the power stroke.

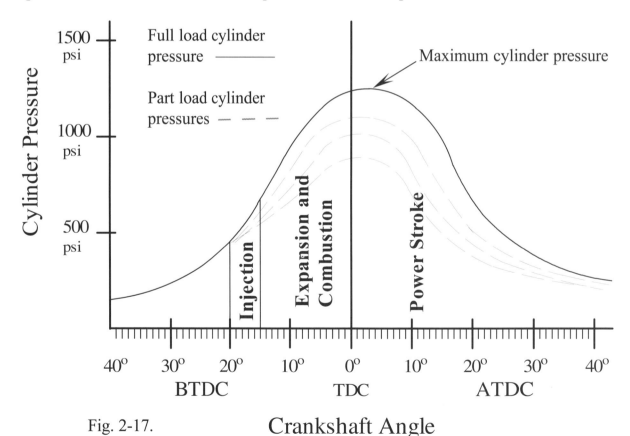

Fig. 2-17.   Crankshaft Angle
(Piston on compression stroke)

Metering (Measuring)

An inline injection pump must deliver a pressurized charge of fuel at precisely the right time to the appropriate engine cylinder. The third task of the fuel system is to measure that amount of fuel for delivery. The amount of fuel being delivered changes for a variety of reasons. The fuel system controls how much fuel will be delivered for any working moment. The dashed lines in Figure 2-17 represent the cylinder pressures created at part load deliveries. Less fuel delivery creates less expansion, less cylinder pressure, and less power.

Figure 2-18 shows two P&Bs at port closing (start of injection) and port opening (end of injection). Refer to Figures 2-3 through 2-7, pages 12-13. The movement of the plunger from port closing to port opening is called the effective stroke. With a slight rotation of the plunger on the right, the helix uncovers the charge port earlier, thus decreasing fuel delivery. All P&Bs in an inline injection pump are connected by a mechanical 'rack' or control rod which changes the rotational position of all plungers uniformly by turning the plunger foot (see Fig. 2-19, p. 20). A change in rack position changes the effective stroke of all the plungers in the injection pump, which changes fuel delivery to all cylinders. Rack movement is precisely controlled by the governor.

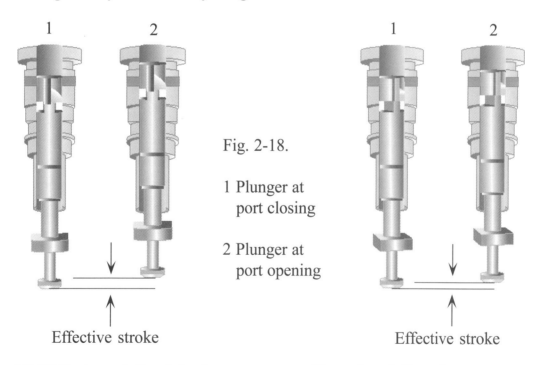

Fig. 2-18.

1 Plunger at port closing

2 Plunger at port opening

Effective stroke   Effective stroke

All P&Bs in an inline injection pump are calibrated to deliver the same amount of fuel within manufacturer's tolerance for the same rack position. The P&Bs for each cylinder create injection pressure at the correct engine crankshaft angle and piston position by means of a camshaft (see Figs. 2-2, p.11 and 2-8, p.14). Adjustment of the timing of injection for each P&B is called phasing. A properly phased inline injection pump delivers fuel to every engine cylinder at the correct piston position. Pressurization of the fuel is not adjustable. The same hydraulic fit of each P&B gives uniform pressurization.

Fig. 2-19. Plungers from a four-cylinder inline injection pump with number two plunger moving up to create injection pressure for engine cylinder number two.

1 Rack or control rod
2 Plunger
3 Control sleeve
4 Roller tappet
5 Camshaft lobe
6 Camshaft

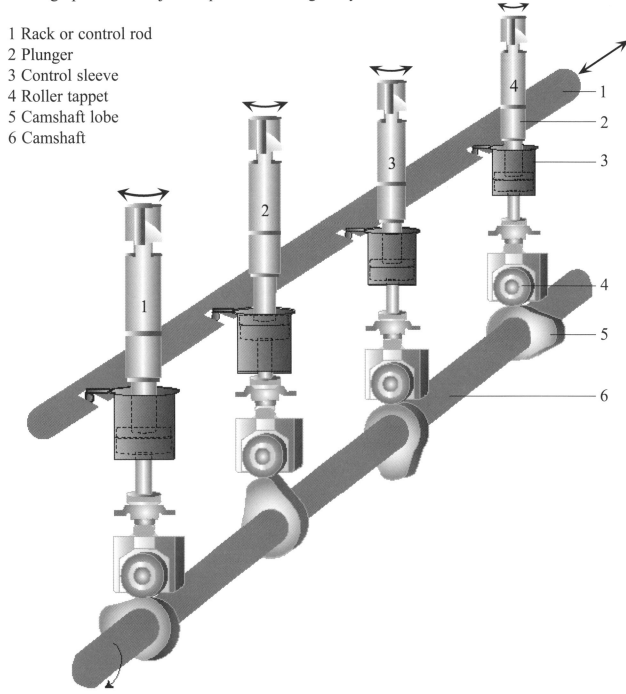

The rack or control rod is connected to the governor. The governor moves the rack to turn the control sleeves and precisely control the rotational position of all the plungers. Changing the rotational position of all the plungers changes the effective stroke of all the P&Bs, thus precisely controlling fuel delivery. For an inline injection pump, total rack movement is usually 21 millimeters (mm). Within the space of 21mm, the governor precisely moves the rack to control fuel metering for all engine-operating conditions.

Distributor injection pump

Fig. 2-20. Distributor (rotary) injection pump with end view of hydraulic head, fuel inlet, and injection line fittings.

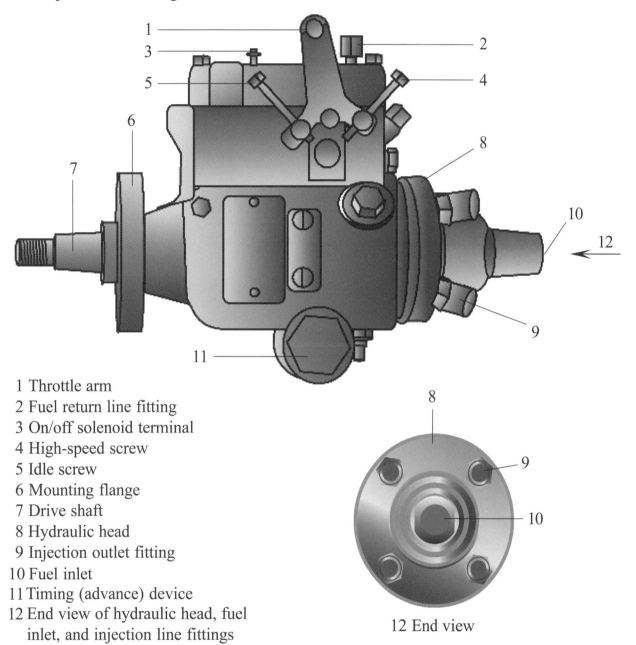

1 Throttle arm
2 Fuel return line fitting
3 On/off solenoid terminal
4 High-speed screw
5 Idle screw
6 Mounting flange
7 Drive shaft
8 Hydraulic head
9 Injection outlet fitting
10 Fuel inlet
11 Timing (advance) device
12 End view of hydraulic head, fuel
   inlet, and injection line fittings

12 End view

Fig. 2-20 illustrates a four-cylinder Stanadyne (Roosa Master) distributor injection pump. A drive gear or drive adapter attached to the pump drive shaft is driven by the engine. The pumping unit (hydraulic head and rotor) is quite different from the P&B, but the function is the same. Just like a P&B, a hydraulic head and rotor must pressurize, time, and meter fuel delivery.

The hydraulic head and rotor creates pressure by a process of high-speed hydraulic pumping. The central rotating member, the rotor, is fitted to the hydraulic head to a tolerance of approximately fifty millionths of an inch. The pumping plungers are fitted to the rotor with the same tolerance. The oiliness, or lubricity, of the diesel fuel is the head and rotor's only lubrication. Fig. 2-21 is a simplified version of the head and rotor and is similar to the pumping unit for a Lucas-CAV model DPA distributor injection pump.

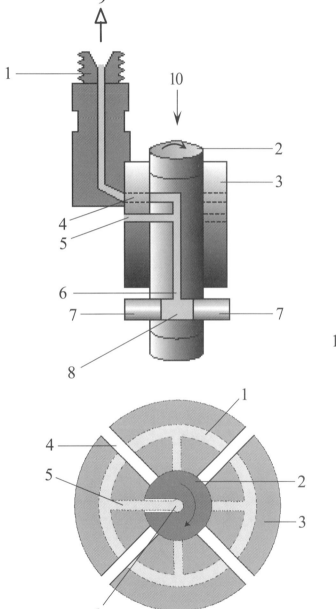

Fig. 2-21.
Cut-away view of
hydraulic head and rotor.

1 Injection outlet fitting
2 Rotor
3 Hydraulic head
4 Discharge port
5 Charge port
6 Charge/discharge passage
7 Pumping plunger
8 Pumping chamber
9 Column of fuel to injector
10 Top cut-away view of Fig. 2-22

Fig. 2-22.
Top cut-away view of a four-cylinder head and rotor during charging cycle.

1 Charging annulus
2 Rotor
3 Hydraulic head
4 Discharge port
5 Charge port
6 Charge/discharge passage

The hydraulic head and rotor is constructed with the charge and discharge ports evenly staggered. As the rotor revolves, the charge/discharge passage indexes (aligns) alternately with the charge and discharge ports. An internal regulated supply pump (or transfer pump) provides fuel pressure to the charging annulus up to 130 psi.

The head and rotor creates pressure by pushing against a column of fuel in the injection line, which pushes against the injector connected to the other end of the injection line. When the injection line pressure reaches the opening pressure of the injector, the injector nozzle opens and delivers an atomized amount of fuel into the combustion chamber. The sequence of operation for a hydraulic head and rotor is:

Pressurizing

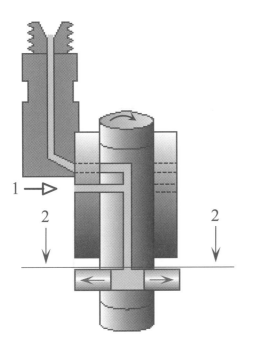

Fig. 2-23.
Cut-away view of hydraulic head and rotor during charging cycle.

1 Fuel pressure from charging annulus
2 Top cut-away view of Fig. 2-24

As the rotor revolves and the charge/discharge passage indexes with the charge port, fuel pressure from the charging annulus pushes the pumping plungers apart and charges (fills) the pumping chamber with fuel.

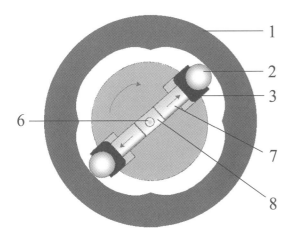

Fig. 2-24.
Top cut-away view of pumping plungers, pumping chamber, and cam ring during charging cycle.

1 Cam ring
2 Roller
3 Shoe
6 Charge/discharge passage
7 Pumping plunger
8 Pumping chamber

The cam ring is fixed in the injection pump housing. As the rotor revolves, the rollers strike the lobes of the cam ring to quickly compress the pumping plungers.

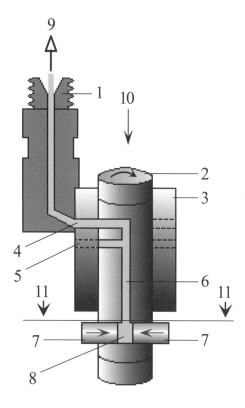

Fig. 2-25.
Cut-away view of hydraulic head and rotor during injection cycle.

1 Injection outlet fitting
2 Rotor
3 Hydraulic head
4 Discharge port
5 Charge port
6 Charge/discharge passage
7 Pumping plunger
8 Pumping chamber
9 Column of fuel to injector
10 Top cut-away view of Fig. 2-27
11 Top cut-away view of Fig. 2-26

The rollers striking the cam ring lobes compress the pumping plungers to create injection pressure as the charge/discharge passage indexes with the discharge port.

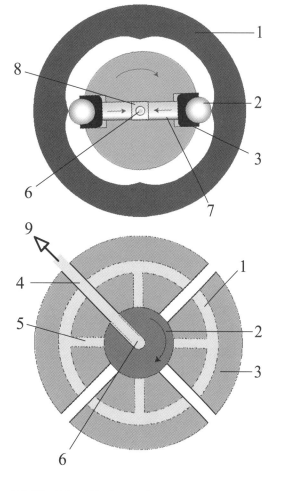

Fig. 2-26.
Top cut-away view of pumping plungers, pumping chamber, and cam ring during injection cycle.

1 Cam ring
2 Roller
3 Shoe
6 Charge/discharge passage
7 Pumping plunger
8 Pumping chamber

Fig. 2-27.
Top cut-away view of a four-cylinder head and rotor during injection cycle.

1 Charging annulus
2 Rotor
3 Hydraulic head
4 Discharge port
5 Charge port
6 Charge/discharge passage
9 Column of fuel to injector

During the charging cycle, fuel pressure from the charging annulus pushes the pumping plungers apart and charges the pumping chamber with fuel. The rotor revolves slightly and closes the charge port. The rotor revolves further and the rollers strike the lobes of the cam ring to quickly compress the pumping plungers. Fuel pressurization for injection begins at this point. The rotor continues to turn and the charge/discharge passage aligns with the discharge port and pushes against the column of fuel in the injection line towards the injector. Injection pressure is created quickly and the injector nozzle opens and delivers an atomized burst of fuel into the engine cylinder. Injection continues until the rotor revolves further and closes the discharge port. After the discharge port is closed, the injection pressure quickly subsides and the injector needle valve snaps shut, ending injection.

After injection, the rotor revolves further, the next charge port aligns with the charge/discharge passage, and the pumping plungers are charged again for the next injection cycle.

Timing

In a pump/line/injector system with a distributor injection pump, each engine cylinder has its own corresponding injector and injection line. The head and rotor supplies fuel to all engine cylinders. Each injection pump outlet must deliver fuel to its corresponding engine cylinder at the correct time. Depending on the engine, delivery occurs for each cylinder between $10°$ BTDC and $40°$ BTDC on the compression stroke.

The head and rotor creates injection pressure for each outlet consecutively in a circular pattern. In the examples we've been using, the rotor turns clockwise looking at the injection outlets.

Fig. 2-28.
End-view of injection outlets.

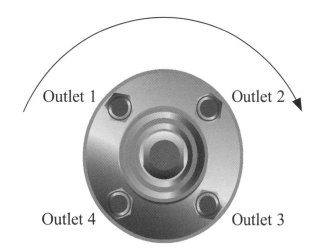

Keep in mind that injection pump rotation is always defined by the rotation of the injection pump drive shaft while looking at the drive end of the injection pump. For this example, since the rotor turns clockwise looking at the injection outlets, the injection pump turns counter-clockwise looking at the drive end and is considered a counter-clockwise pump (see Fig. 2-20, p. 21).

A common firing order for a four-cylinder engine is 1-3-4-2. For a diesel engine with a distributor injection pump, the routing of the injection lines determines the firing order for the injection pump, just as the routing of spark plug wires determines the firing order for a distributor in a gasoline engine.

When the piston in engine cylinder number one is near the top of the compression stroke, head and rotor outlet number one creates injection pressure and the injector delivers fuel into the engine cylinder's hot compressed air. When the piston in engine cylinder number three is near the top of the compression stroke, head and rotor outlet number two creates injection pressure and the injector delivers fuel as the injection line for cylinder number three is connected to head and rotor outlet number two. Head and rotor outlet number three delivers fuel for cylinder number four and outlet number four delivers fuel for cylinder number two.

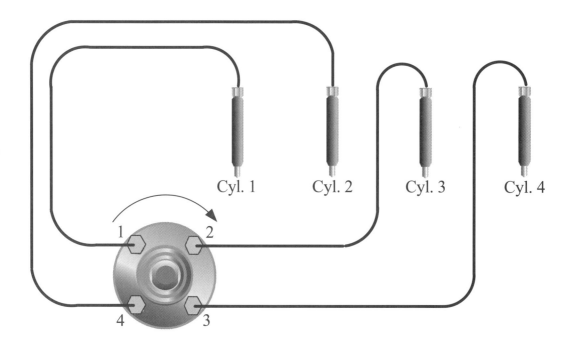

Fig. 2-29.
Routing of injection lines for a four-cylinder engine with a 1-3-4-2 firing order.

A distributor injection pump may have one or more timing devices to advance or retard the timing of injection for certain factors. For any working moment, the fuel injection system injects the fuel at the right time to burn all the fuel as completely as possible and make the maximum cylinder pressure occur just after TDC, which creates optimum power (see Fig. 2-17, p. 18).

Metering (Measuring)

A distributor injection pump must deliver a pressurized charge of fuel at the right time to the appropriate engine cylinder. The third task of the injection pump is to measure that amount of fuel for delivery.

The hydraulic head and rotor is supplied with internal transfer pump pressure through the charging annulus during the charging cycle (see Fig. 2-23, p. 23). As the engine revolutions per minute (RPMs) increase and the injection pump turns faster, the time that the charge port is aligned with the charge/discharge passage decreases. Since the time available for charging the pumping plungers is decreased, internal transfer pump pressure must increase by way of the charging annulus as engine RPM increases to maintain full load delivery. Fig. 2-24, p. 23 illustrates charging for full load or maximum fuel delivery.

A Stanadyne or Lucas-CAV distributor injection pump meters fuel delivery by restricting the internal transfer pump pressure in the charging annulus by means of a metering valve. With less charge pressure, the pumping plungers are not pushed apart as far and less fuel fills the pumping chamber. Fig. 2-30 compares a full-load charge cycle and a part-load charge cycle.

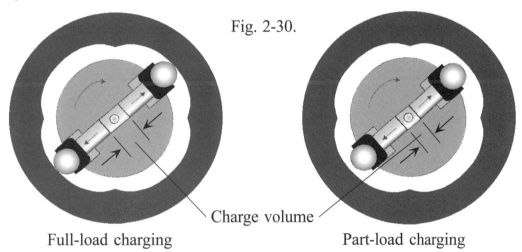

Fig. 2-30.

Charge volume

Full-load charging   Part-load charging

Since the pumping chamber is filled with less fuel during a part-load charging cycle, when the rotor turns and begins the injection cycle, less fuel is displaced when the pumping plungers are compressed and less fuel is injected (see Fig. 2-26, p. 24).

Movement of the metering valve is precisely controlled by the injection pump governor by means of a control rod or governor arm. A change in the metering valve position changes the annulus charge pressure, which changes the amount of fuel that fills the pumping chamber during the charging cycle. By this process, fuel delivery to all engine cylinders is precisely controlled.

A Stanadyne or Lucas-CAV head and rotor has an adjustable device (not shown) that limits the maximum travel of the shoes and rollers, thus controlling maximum fuel delivery. Maximum or full-load fuel delivery is set to specification during pump calibration.

Equality of timing and fuel delivery between cylinders is an inherent quality of the hydraulic head and rotor because of the accurate spacing of the charge and discharge ports in the hydraulic head.

Governing

The correct amount of metered fuel produces the appropriate amount of power. For any amount of power developed by the engine, an opposing force called 'load' counters this power. Fuel systems react to engine speed, power requirements, and load in different ways to increase or decrease fuel delivery as needed. Precise metering of fuel delivery is critical for the engine to run smoothly, to run clean, and to meet its power requirements.

The process by which the fuel system reacts and regulates the amount of metered fuel is called governing and the device that accomplishes governing is called a governor. The governor precisely controls the amount of fuel metered for startup, idle, full load, high idle, and high-speed cutoff. The operator of the engine usually controls the other part-load requirements by means of an accelerator or throttle device.

Diesel governors are generally very reliable. Quite often, air-in-fuel (air ingress) and other fuel supply problems are mistakenly blamed on the governor. This topic is discussed further in Chapter 5.

Although the types and variations of governors are numerous, they can be divided into four basic categories; mechanical, hydraulic, pneumatic, and electronic. Mechanical governors utilize flyweights and springs to precisely regulate rack or control rod movements for all engine RPMs and throttle positions. Hydraulic governors use fuel pressure (internal transfer pump pressure) to move governor parts and regulate fuel delivery. Pneumatic governors use intake manifold vacuum to control rack position. Electronic governors incorporate an electronic servo mechanism to precisely regulate rack or control rod movements. Every diesel engine application has its governor engineered and calibrated for a specific purpose.

The following graph, Fig. 2-31, illustrates typical governor regulation of fuel delivery versus engine speed for a common fuel injection system in a non-turbocharged (naturally aspirated) diesel tractor. Fuel delivery is described as the amount of fuel delivered per injection in cubic millimeters per stroke (mm³/str). 1000 cubic millimeters equals 1 cubic centimeter (cm³ or cc). 1000 cubic centimeters equals 1 liter. Engine speed is described as RPM.

The area inside the graph (Fig. 2-31, position 11) shows the part-load deliveries that the operator controls by means of a throttle device or accelerator.

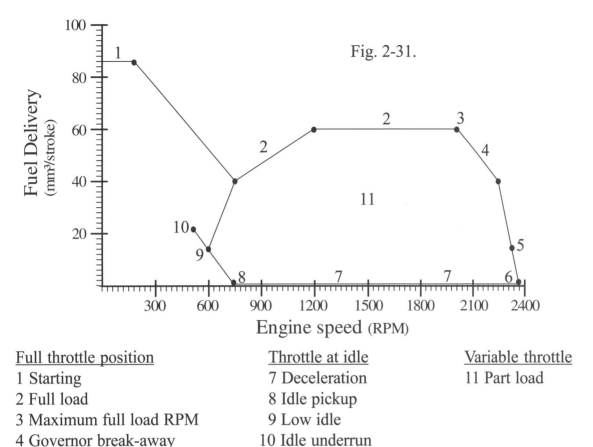

Fig. 2-31.

Full throttle position
1 Starting
2 Full load
3 Maximum full load RPM
4 Governor break-away
5 High idle
6 Governor cutoff

Throttle at idle
7 Deceleration
8 Idle pickup
9 Low idle
10 Idle underrun

Variable throttle
11 Part load

At graph position 1, the starter turns the engine at approximately 200 RPM. The fuel system delivers a large amount of fuel per injection for easy starting. Once the engine starts, if the operator moves the throttle to idle, the fuel delivery and RPM decrease to position 9 and the engine idles at 600 RPM. While the engine is working under load, the engine runs at positions 2, 3, and 11. If the tractor has to overcome a heavy load, the operator works the engine at positions 2 and 3. More fuel delivery means more power.

This particular engine is rated for a maximum full load of 2000 RPM. At full throttle, the fuel system governor only allows full fuel delivery up to 2000 RPM. Beyond 2000 RPM, the governor begins to cut back the fuel delivery.

If no load is applied to the tractor and the operator accelerates the engine from idle with the throttle at full, the engine RPM increases to positions 4 and 5. Position 5 is the maximum no-load RPM or high idle, in this case about 2300 RPM. It is not recommended to run an engine at high idle unless necessary for the application. Returning the throttle to the idle position reduces fuel delivery to zero or close to zero (position 7) and the engine decelerates. At 750 RPM, the fuel system begins to deliver fuel again (position 8) to begin slowing the deceleration. If the momentum from deceleration carries the engine below 600 RPM (position 9), the governor increases fuel delivery to correct the 'underrun' (position 10), and brings the engine back up to 600 RPM.

Injectors

You now understand the concept of the high-speed, high-pressure pumping action of the injection pump and the role of the governor to control and regulate fuel metering. The other part of the fuel system, the injector, must work together with the injection pump to take the pressurized, metered charge of fuel and deliver it to the combustion chamber at the right time and under the right conditions. Since the injection pump controls the pressurization, timing, and metering of fuel, the injector must atomize and distribute the fuel properly. The quick burst of fuel pressure from the injection pump overcomes the preload force of the injector spring, which is set between 1500 psi and 5000 psi for different engines and applications. The pressure created by the pumping unit, transferred through the injection line, overcomes the preload force of the injector spring and lifts the needle valve off its seat. Then, once the needle valve opens, the burst of injection pressure forces fuel through very small holes in the nozzle tip. A burst of pressure forcing fuel through very small holes, .005 to .015 of an inch in diameter, allows injection pressure to increase during injection.

The injector spring preload force is adjusted with a screw device or by changing the thickness of the injector spring shim. Fig. 2-32 shows a typical shim-adjusted injector. Injector opening pressures are set to manufacturer's specifications and all injectors in an engine must be set to the same opening pressure within tolerance, usually plus or minus 50 psi. A common injector opening pressure is 2500 psi.

Depending on the system, injection pressures range from 2000 psi to 25,000 psi. The extremely high injection pressure happens for just a few milliseconds and creates a finely atomized burst of fuel delivered into the hot compressed air of the combustion chamber. The number of spray holes in the nozzle tip properly distribute the fuel in the direction in which the spray holes are pointing. After the pressure burst from the injection pump subsides, the preload force of the injector spring snaps the needle valve shut and delivery quickly ends. Fig. 2-33, p. 32 illustrates injection pressure and corresponding crankshaft angle for a common inline injection pump/injection line/injector system. The graph in Fig. 2-33 can also represent injection pressure for a distributor injection pump.

Injection lines are engineered as part of the injection pump and injector system. The thick-walled steel tubing transfers the injection pressure created by the pumping unit to the injector. Most injection lines have conically-shaped ends with line nuts to make a complete high-pressure seal at the injection pump and injector.

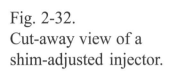

1 →

Fig. 2-32.
Cut-away view of a
shim-adjusted injector.

1 Column of fuel pressure from
  injection pump
2 Injection line
3 Injection line nut
4 High-pressure passageway
5 Injector return fuel to tank
6 Injector spring adjusting shim
7 Injector spring
8 Injector spring spindle
9 Nozzle (valve) assembly
10 Needle valve
11 Nozzle spray hole
12 Nozzle valve seat

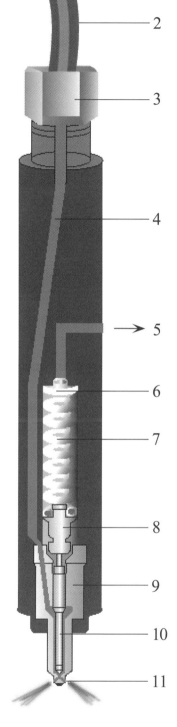

Needle valve open during injection

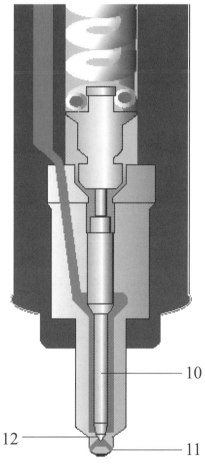

Needle valve closed

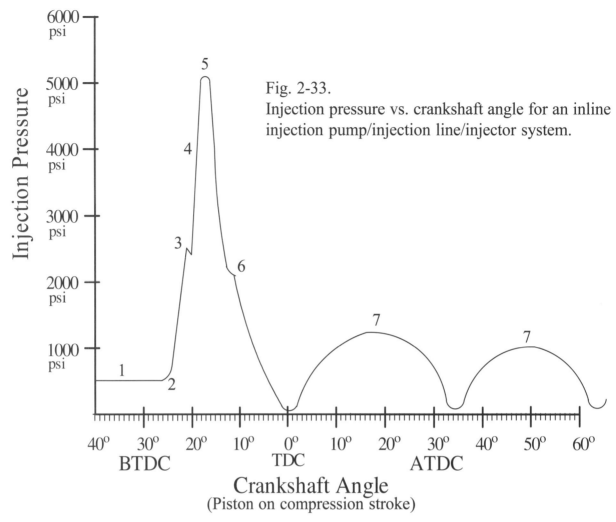

Fig. 2-33.
Injection pressure vs. crankshaft angle for an inline injection pump/injection line/injector system.

1 Residual injection line pressure from previous injection cycle.

2 P&B at port closing, start of pressurization. See Fig. 2-5, p. 13.

3 Start of injection. Injection pressure reaches the opening pressure of the injector, in this case 2500 psi. The injection pressure overcomes the preload force of the injector spring and lifts the needle valve off its seat. See Figs. 2-6, p. 13 and 2-32, p. 31. A slight dip in pressure occurs as the fuel pressure begins forcing through the injector nozzle spray holes.

4 Injection. See Fig. 2-17, p. 18. Injection pressure continues to rise as fuel is being forced through the injector nozzle spray holes. The amount of fuel delivered is controlled by the governor which regulates the metering of the plunger and barrel. See Figs. 2-18, p. 19 and 2-31, p. 29.

5 Port opening. See Fig. 2-7, p. 13. The P&B has moved through the effective stroke and begins to relieve the injection pressure.

6 End of injection. The injection pressure drops quickly and the injector spring snaps the needle valve shut.

7 Afterwaves. Injection happens so quickly that residual pressure waves bounce back and forth between the injector and injection pump. The fuel injection system is engineered to keep the maximum pressure from the reflected waves below the injector opening pressure to prevent secondary injection.

With the three tasks of the injection pump accomplished; *i.e.*, pressurization, timing, and metering of fuel, the injector delivers a high-pressure, atomized burst of fuel into the engine cylinder's hot compressed air. This causes the fuel to expand and burn completely, creating tremendous cylinder pressure that forces the piston down. This power is transferred from the piston by means of a connecting rod to the crankshaft. The power coming from the crankshaft is used to overcome a certain amount of load. The fuel system governor or operator controls more or less fuel delivery for any working moment.

Although the types and variations of fuel injection systems are numerous, they all have a commonality. Any type of diesel fuel injection system must pressurize, time, and meter fuel for delivery and the injector or nozzle must properly atomize and distribute the fuel into the engine cylinder's hot compressed air.

Now that we've covered the basic theory of a diesel engine and fuel system, let's take a close look at the most misunderstood aspect of the process, expansion and combustion.

Chapter 3 - Expansion and Combustion

You now know that a diesel engine piston quickly compresses an amount of air, creating very high temperature. The fuel system injects a pressurized, timed, and metered amount of fuel into the combustion chamber. The expansion and combustion create cylinder pressure that forces the piston down for the power stroke.

Understanding how the atomized diesel fuel expands and burns is your first key to saving money. So much is misunderstood about the diesel combustion process and a great deal of money is spent on unnecessary repairs. This Chapter and Chapter 4 will clear up all the mysteries.

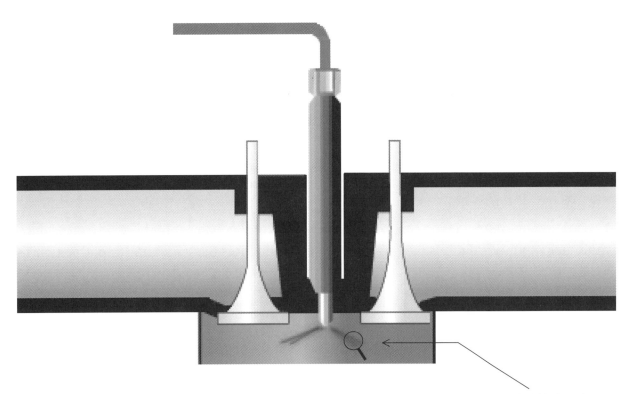

Fig. 3-1. Injection at 20° BTDC on compression stroke. Fig. 3-2 shows the highlighted area of the atomized fuel.

When the atomized diesel fuel hits the hot compressed air in the combustion chamber, the first thing that happens is that the atomized diesel fuel vaporizes, changes into a white colored fuel vapor and expands. The expansion of the white fuel vapor accounts for as much as 80% of the total cylinder pressure created.

Fig. 3-2.
Magnified view of atomized diesel fuel from Fig. 3-1.

Fig. 3-3.
Atomized diesel fuel vaporizes and changes into a white fuel vapor.

Vaporization and expansion happen instantly when the atomized fuel hits the hot compressed air. Combustion begins because the vaporized diesel fuel has plenty of heat and oxygen available. Since injection occurs over 4-6 crankshaft degrees (see Fig. 2-17, p. 18), the fuel injected at 20° BTDC vaporizes, expands, and begins to burn while the last amount of fuel injected at 16° BTDC begins to vaporize and expand. If the injection timing is correct, all of the injected fuel will have time to vaporize, expand, and burn completely. The expansion created by combustion, or the burning of the white fuel vapor, accounts for the rest of the pressure created in the cylinder. Upon vaporization and expansion of the atomized diesel fuel, the heat, oxygen, and fuel vapor present in the cylinder combine and create a mini-explosion. The expansion and combustion process happens in milliseconds. Combustion occurs like an exploding firecracker. The inherent clattering sound created by a diesel engine is the sound of the continuous combustion explosions that power the engine.

The important point to remember is that the atomized diesel fuel initially turns into a white fuel vapor when it hits the hot compressed air and it is the white fuel vapor that burns. A common misconception is that combustion occurs before expansion. However, the opposite is true. Most of the expansion that creates the cylinder pressure is caused by the vaporization and expansion of the atomized diesel fuel. Then combustion creates the rest of the cylinder pressure that forces the piston down.

It should be noted that, unlike a gasoline engine, a diesel engine can have excess air (oxygen) present in the cylinder at the time of injection. The metered and atomized fuel that is injected into the cylinder uses the amount of oxygen necessary for combustion. Any extra oxygen present has no effect on the combustion process.

Three components are necessary to create proper expansion and combustion in a diesel engine: fuel; heat; and oxygen. When an engine is not starting or running correctly, the exhaust, exhaust color, or lack of exhaust can tell you what components necessary for combustion might be missing.

Fuel plus Heat minus Oxygen. Diesel fuel injected at the correct time with proper heat present, but without sufficient oxygen, creates black exhaust. The greater the air restriction, the worse the engine will run with heavier black exhaust, or not run at all. Although black exhaust is caused by other factors as well, removing oxygen from the equation is a common cause.

Fuel plus Oxygen minus Heat. Diesel fuel injected at the correct time with sufficient oxygen present but without enough heat creates white exhaust, as in a low compression problem. The atomized fuel makes the first step and turns into a white fuel vapor and expands, but insufficient heat is present to cause complete combustion. Diesel fuel injected too late (retarded timing) with sufficient oxygen will create white exhaust as well because the white fuel vapor doesn't have enough time to burn. White exhaust situations are caused by timing, low compression, or cold engine problems.

Heat plus Oxygen minus Fuel. An engine cannot run without fuel. An engine that doesn't start and makes no visible exhaust means that no fuel is being injected.

When all of the variables are correct, a diesel engine should start easily, have minimal white exhaust while warming up, supply the appropriate power for the application, and run clean during all modes of operation.

Indirect injection or prechamber engines

The engine cylinders shown so far represent a direct injection diesel engine. Diesel fuel is injected directly into the combustion chamber (see Fig. 3-1, p. 35). Another variation of engine design is the indirect injection engine or prechamber engine. A small prechamber is machined into the head with a passage to the combustion chamber. Expansion and combustion begin in the prechamber and the expansion created moves to the cylinder to force the piston down. The primary reason for a prechamber engine design is to reduce the noise of combustion. Many diesel passenger cars have prechamber engines.

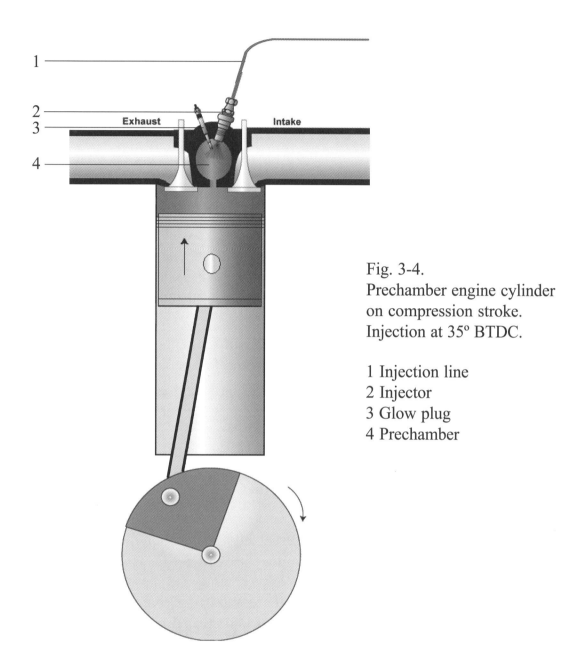

Fig. 3-4.
Prechamber engine cylinder
on compression stroke.
Injection at 35° BTDC.

1 Injection line
2 Injector
3 Glow plug
4 Prechamber

The four-stroke cycle for a prechamber diesel engine is the same as for a direct injection engine. See Figs. 1-5 through 1-8, pages 6-7.

Combustion noise is reduced in the prechamber engine because the combustion process is slowed down. The atomized fuel is injected into the hot compressed air in the prechamber and expands and burns as previously described, but the prechamber creates a swirling effect, which slows down the process and dampens the noise a bit. Consequently, a slower burning process requires higher compression to maintain the appropriate heat for the expansion and combustion process. Prechamber engines have a higher compression ratio than direct injection engines, up to 25 to 1. A typical compression ratio for a direct injection engine is 15 to 1. Since the expansion and combustion process is slower in a prechamber engine, start-of-injection timing is earlier than in the direct injection engine in order for the maximum cylinder pressure from combustion to occur at the optimum point, just after TDC. Prechamber engines can usually be identified by a glow plug in the head for each cylinder. Glow plugs are used to preheat the cylinder for start-up only.

Figure 3-5 shows the relationship between cylinder pressure and crankshaft angle for a prechamber diesel engine cylinder on the compression and power strokes. Compared to the same graph for a direct injection engine (see Fig. 2-17, p. 18), the prechamber engine has made more compression at 40° BTDC than the direct injection engine due to the higher compression ratio.

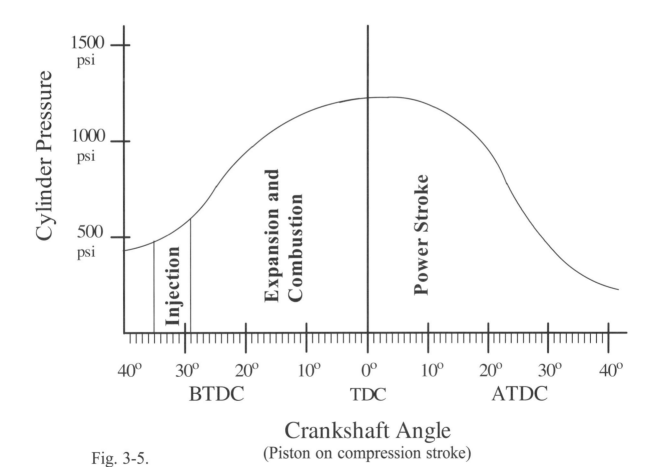

Fig. 3-5. Crankshaft Angle
(Piston on compression stroke)

Comparing the charts in Fig. 2-17, p. 18 and Fig. 3-5, p. 39, you can see that the expansion and combustion process for the direct injection engine occurs faster than for the prechamber engine. The combustion mini-explosion in the prechamber engine occurs more slowly and creates less noise.

Timing devices

Many diesel fuel injection systems incorporate one or more timing devices. Timing devices are used to compensate for changes in engine speed, load, and other factors, which affect the expansion and combustion process. For any engine speed, load, and throttle position, timing devices are calibrated to advance or retard the injection timing throughout the operating range as needed so that all the fuel will burn as completely as possible and make the maximum cylinder pressure occur just after TDC.

Speed advance is the most common timing compensation in a fuel injection system. As a diesel engine accelerates and moves faster and faster, the time available for pressurization and injection to occur becomes shorter and shorter. Since the injection process occurs over a fixed amount of time, a natural retardation effect occurs, called injection lag. Without a timing change at higher RPMs, injection occurs later as engine RPM increases. Injection lag in a diesel engine is similar to ignition lag in a gasoline engine. Using the chart from Figure 2-17, p. 18, injection begins at 20° BTDC. For this example, the engine is running at 1000 RPM.

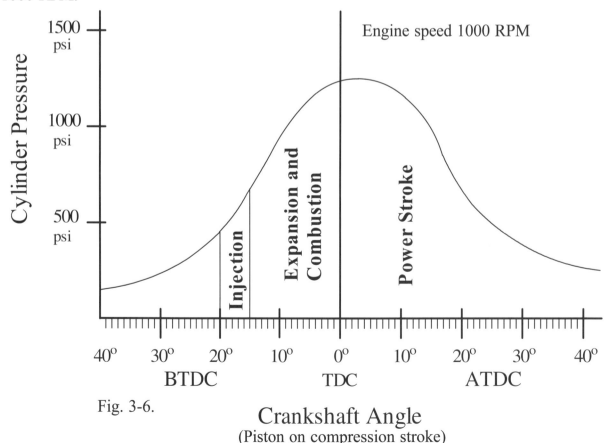

Fig. 3-6.

Crankshaft Angle
(Piston on compression stroke)

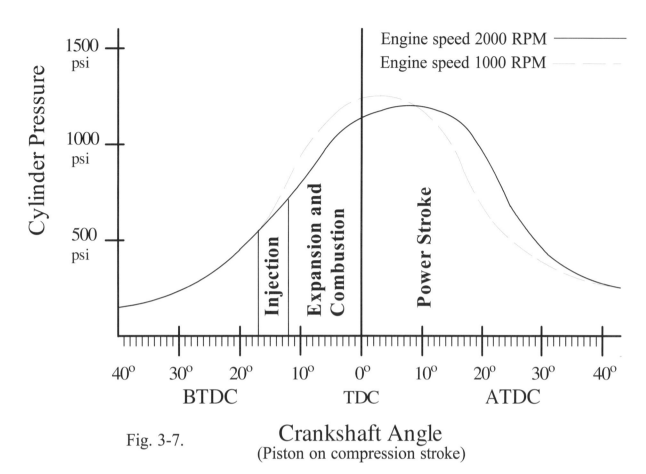

Fig. 3-7.

Crankshaft Angle
(Piston on compression stroke)

At 2000 RPM, start of injection occurs at 17° BTDC due to injection lag, compared to 20° BTDC at 1000 RPM. The fuel injected into the cylinder doesn't have enough time to expand and burn completely to make the maximum cylinder pressure occur just after TDC. Without a timing adjustment at 2000 RPM, the maximum cylinder pressure happens about 6° later than at 1000 RPM.

The timing device solves the problem of injection lag by gradually advancing the injection timing between 1000 RPM and 2000 RPM.

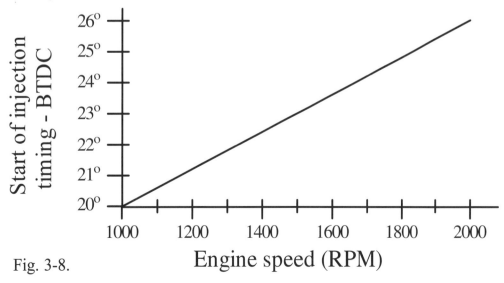

Fig. 3-8.

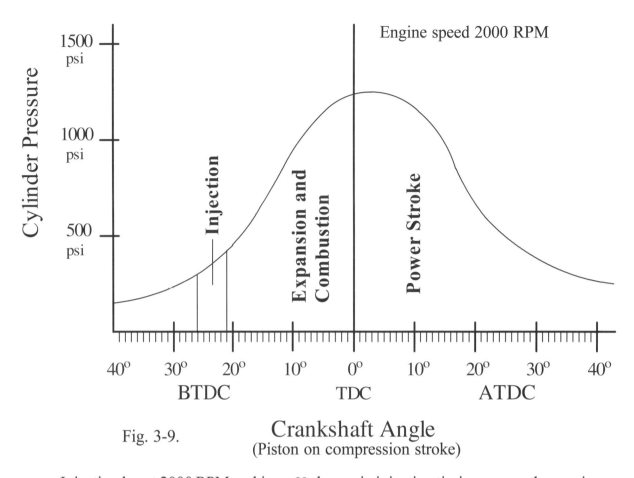

Fig. 3-9.
Crankshaft Angle
(Piston on compression stroke)

Injection lag at 2000 RPM making a 3° change in injection timing causes the maximum cylinder pressure to occur 6° later than at 1000 RPM because another factor is at work. The time needed for expansion and combustion to occur is also fixed. The time available for expansion and combustion to occur is cut in half at 2000 RPM compared to 1000 RPM. A natural retardation effect takes place as the engine accelerates. At 2000 RPM, this combustion lag effect combined with injection lag causes the maximum cylinder pressure to occur 6° later than at 1000 RPM. A speed-advance timing device compensates for both injection lag and combustion lag. With the engine running at 2000 RPM and start-of-injection timing at 26° BTDC, the expansion and combustion process has the time needed to burn the fuel completely and make the maximum cylinder pressure happen just after TDC. A similar condition takes place in a gasoline engine. An advance device in the distributor compensates for ignition lag and combustion lag to make ignition advance (happen sooner) at higher engine RPMs.

Many diesel fuel injection systems incorporate one or more timing devices to compensate for injection lag, combustion lag, and other factors that affect the expansion and combustion process throughout the operating range of the engine. Light-load advance, altitude advance, start retard, start advance, and idle advance are some of the other types of timing devices that fine-tune a diesel engine. For any working moment, engine speed, operating condition, and load, the timing devices will adjust the start-of-injection timing to its optimum point. This type of precision makes diesel engines run very clean and efficiently.

Power and load

The correct amount of metered fuel produces the appropriate amount of power. For any amount of power developed by the engine, an opposing force called 'load' counters this power. Load is the combination of all forces opposing the power produced by the engine. When more load is applied to an engine, the engine slows down. To maintain the power to carry an additional load, the operator or fuel system governor must control the fuel metering to deliver more fuel. When less load is applied to an engine, the engine speeds up. To maintain the power for a lesser load, the operator or fuel system governor must control the fuel metering to deliver less fuel.

Different types of equipment powered by diesel engines are designed to overcome different types of load and are equipped with different governors for their particular tasks. A tractor has to overcome different types of load than a car or boat, but the basic concept of power and load is the same. Figures 3-10 through 3-14 illustrate the power/load relationship for a diesel powered automobile.

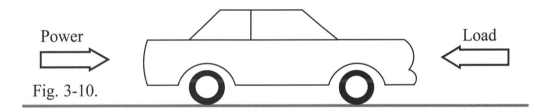

Fig. 3-10.

For an automobile traveling at 55 miles per hour (MPH), the engine creates just enough power to counter all of the load that is opposing the engine. Load includes mechanical friction through the engine and drive train, load from engine accessories, road friction from the tires, gross vehicle weight, and wind resistance.

Fig. 3-11.

If the automobile starts climbing a hill, the load on the vehicle increases and the vehicle and engine start to slow down. For the automobile to continue traveling at 55 MPH, the driver must press on the accelerator so that the fuel system will deliver more fuel and the engine will develop more power to handle the extra load.

Fig. 3-12.

If the automobile starts going down a hill, the load on the vehicle decreases and the vehicle and engine start to speed up. For the automobile to continue traveling at 55 MPH, the driver must let up on the accelerator so that the fuel system will deliver less fuel and the engine will develop less power to adjust to the smaller load.

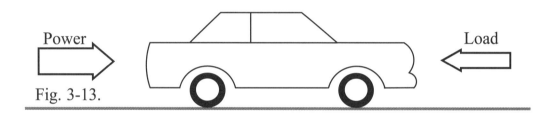
Fig. 3-13.

If the automobile is traveling at 55 MPH, and the driver wants to accelerate to 65 MPH, the driver must press on the accelerator so the fuel system will deliver more fuel and the engine will develop more power to overcome the load already opposing the vehicle and cause the vehicle to accelerate.

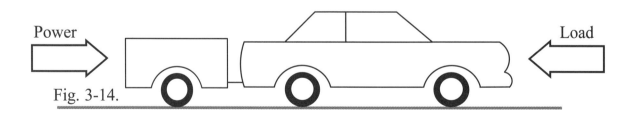
Fig. 3-14.

An automobile pulling a trailer has to develop more power than the previous examples to travel at 55 MPH. The trailer adds weight and road friction to the total load opposing the engine. Since the load is greater, the engine must produce more power to travel at 55 MPH.

These simple examples of the power/load relationship will help you to understand the power/load relationship for any type of diesel equipment.

In a properly running direct injection or prechamber diesel engine, the piston compresses air in the cylinder to make heat. The injection pump pressurizes, times, and meters fuel delivery. The injector nozzle atomizes and distributes the fuel into the cylinder or prechamber. Timing devices may adjust the start-of-injection timing so that the expansion and combustion process occurs at the optimum time. Expansion and combustion commence to make cylinder pressure, which forces the piston down for the power stroke. More fuel delivery creates more cylinder pressure by creating more expansion and greater combustion, and hence more power. Power developed by the engine is countered by load. The governor or the operator controls the fuel metering for any working moment to increase, decrease, or maintain an amount of power working against load.

When all the variables are correct, a diesel engine should start easily, have minimal white exhaust while warming up, and little or no visible exhaust when operating. Now that you have a good understanding of the diesel engine, let's start changing the variables and solve some runability problems.

Chapter 4 - Exhaust, the Key to Troubleshooting

People generally associate diesel exhaust with the belching black smoke of city buses, or the black clouds pouring from a trucker's exhaust stack. We really don't pay much attention to a diesel engine that puts out little to no visible exhaust, but those are the engines that are well maintained and are running properly.

Unlike gasoline engines, if a diesel engine's exhaust looks clean, then the engine is running clean and burning the fuel properly and completely. When a diesel engine is not running properly, the color and type of exhaust will put you on the road to remedy. The exhaust does not always tell you where the problem is coming from, but it puts you on the right track towards a solution. Even if an engine is experiencing a loss of power problem and the exhaust is clean, the exhaust (or lack of it) tells us something.

The troubleshooting charts on pages 139-148 are designed to expand your knowledge of diesel engine and fuel system processes and to supplement any troubleshooting or repair information. They are not intended to replace any service manuals. For the do-it-yourselfers, be sure to read and follow the factory service manual procedures and safety precautions for your particular engine or equipment.

The troubleshooting charts in this handbook list problems, system variations, associated exhaust, and possible causes. For each problem, the possible causes listed first are the easier and less expensive causes. The possible causes progress to the point of fuel injection system or engine repair or replacement. However, before you have an injection pump, injector, or engine repaired or replaced, you will know where the defect is located through proper troubleshooting. Nobody wants to waste time and money having something repaired or replaced unnecessarily. By referencing this handbook, you can often solve runability problems long before expensive components need to be repaired or replaced. And when an injection pump, injector, or engine needs service, you can feel confident that you have checked all other possibilities and that you are spending money wisely on repairs.

Unless otherwise stated, all runability problems described in this handbook use a warmed-up direct injection engine equipped with an injection pump/injection line/injector system in good working order, using suitable fuel under normal working conditions.

Boat owners and boat mechanics may have difficulty troubleshooting an engine problem using the exhaust, as many boats are equipped to deliver the exhaust into the water.

Sometimes a residue of black exhaust can be seen above the water, but it is difficult to discern white fuel exhaust from steam. If the exhaust leaves a film of raw fuel on the water, you can be sure that the exhaust is white. Boat owners and boat mechanics quite often have to use other indicators to troubleshoot engine problems, such as exhaust temperature, engine response, engine power, intermittent surging, etc. However, being able to view the exhaust is the ideal situation.

Loss of power, clean exhaust

A common first response to a low power problem is to have the injection pump and/or injectors tested or repaired. With a pump/line/injector system, the injection pump determines how much fuel is delivered. If the exhaust is clean, you can assume that the injection pump is not delivering enough fuel. Other loss-of-power problems generally cause colored exhaust. The first possibility to check is the movement of the throttle on the injection pump. With the accelerator or throttle linkage at full position, does the throttle arm on the injection pump move fully to hit the high-speed screw? Cables and linkages can wear or stretch with use and eventually fail to move the throttle on the injection pump fully. Usually a linkage adjustment can be made to compensate for this wear. Sometimes cables or other linkage parts must be replaced. Another symptom of a throttle movement problem is that the engine will not develop full RPM.

Fuel injection systems come with mechanical or electric shut-off devices. A mechanical shut-off lever that is partially closed can reduce the amount of fuel the injection pump delivers and cause this problem. Check for proper movement of shut-off levers. Electrical shut-off devices (solenoids) can fail or stick, causing the pump to deliver less fuel as well. Shut-off solenoids can be divided into two categories; energized-to-run (ETR), and energized-to-shut-off (ETSO). Most solenoids are the ETR type and will not work properly without correct and continuous voltage. ETSO solenoids need no electricity for the engine to run. They are energized to stop the engine and are common in marine applications. Some solenoids are part of the injection pump. A solenoid failure does not necessarily mean that the injection pump must be removed. Be sure to obtain service manual procedures to check or replace solenoids. Some solenoids are easy to replace and some are not. Visit your local diesel fuel injection shop for help if needed. If a unit is still under warranty, only authorized service outlets should perform repairs.

Another possible cause of a low power, clean exhaust problem is a restriction in the fuel supply. A dirty fuel filter that needs to be changed causes a restriction. A fuel restriction in the return line of some distributor pumps can cause a loss of power. Depending on the type of fuel system, a fuel supply or fuel return restriction can cause a loss of power with some white or bluish-white exhaust, as the pressure controlled timing device of the injection pump may be affected. Air in the fuel supply can also cause the injection pump to not function correctly, causing low power with clean exhaust or with white exhaust. Air ingress problems can also make the engine run rough, surge, stall, and be hard to start.

More possible causes of this problem are addressed in Chapters 5 and 7 when other related systems are discussed. For now, the last possible cause of loss of power with clean exhaust is a defective injection pump. Fuel systems fail for a variety of reasons and some failures can cause the injection pump to underfuel, or pump less than it is supposed to. If the throttle and shut-off devices are working correctly, the fuel supply and fuel returns are not restricted, the fuel supply is free of air, and the injection pump fuel gallery or pump housing is completely full of fuel, then the problem will be in the injection pump.

Approaching diesel problems this way, by having good knowledge at the start, and eliminating one possible cause after the other, you will find the quickest and least expensive solution to the problem. I mentioned earlier that a common response to low power problems is to first have the injectors tested. Remember that unless the injectors are new or close to new, an injector test will likely show something wrong. The injectors might not spray or chatter as well as new injectors, or the opening pressure could be a little low. These conditions have nothing to do with a low power problem with clean exhaust. Since the injectors are already out of the engine, many customers decide to have the injectors serviced anyway. The new or rebuilt injectors are installed and the low power problem still remains. I have seen entire fuel systems repaired or replaced before someone realized that the throttle linkage wasn't moving the throttle to full position on the injection pump, which caused the entire loss-of-power problem. This situation can be easily avoided by relying upon the good information from this handbook and using a little common sense.

Light to moderate white exhaust, normal power

Again, a common first response to this problem is to have the injectors tested. A defective injector seldom causes white exhaust. When troubleshooting this problem, realize that white exhaust could mean a bluish-white exhaust also, because a small amount of oil may be burning. Light to moderate white exhaust is normal for some engines as they are warming up.

In Chapter 3, you learned that when the high pressure, atomized fuel from the injector nozzle hits the hot compressed air in the combustion chamber, the atomized fuel vaporizes, expands, and becomes a white fuel vapor. It is the white fuel vapor that burns. Whenever you see white exhaust from a diesel engine, you are probably seeing unburned fuel vapor. If a diesel engine expels some white exhaust when starting and while warming up, this is considered normal if the white exhaust clears after the engine has warmed up and is working under load. If the white exhaust doesn't clear after the engine has warmed up and is working, some troubleshooting is needed to find the cause and to correct the problem.

Cold weather can cause white exhaust that is nothing more than steam. When the hot diesel exhaust hits cold air, it can instantly cause condensation and make mist or steam. Excessive white exhaust that dissipates quickly is usually water vapor. Excessive white exhaust that is cloudy, lingers, and has a very strong smell, is unburned fuel vapor. A small amount of white exhaust that is unburned fuel vapor will dissipate quickly.

Water or coolant coming into the combustion chamber from a blown head gasket can make slight to light white exhaust, depending on the amount of water or coolant entering the cylinder. Usually a blown head gasket will become apparent by observing a rough running engine, white exhaust, the loss of coolant, and possibly bubbles in the radiator.

Unless an engine operates in very cold weather or has head gasket problems, once an engine is warmed-up and working, any white exhaust will be unburned fuel vapors. A common cause of light to moderate white exhaust is normal wear of the injection pump and/or the injection pump drive train. Going back to the graph of a cylinder's compression, injection, and combustion process in Fig. 2-17, p. 18, the atomized and then vaporized fuel burns correctly and completely if it has the time to do so. A small amount of lash, or wear on drive gears, drive shafts, etc., can cause the injection timing to occur a little later than normal. It just takes a couple of degrees of retarded (late) timing to cause the last bit of injected fuel to not have the time it needs to burn.

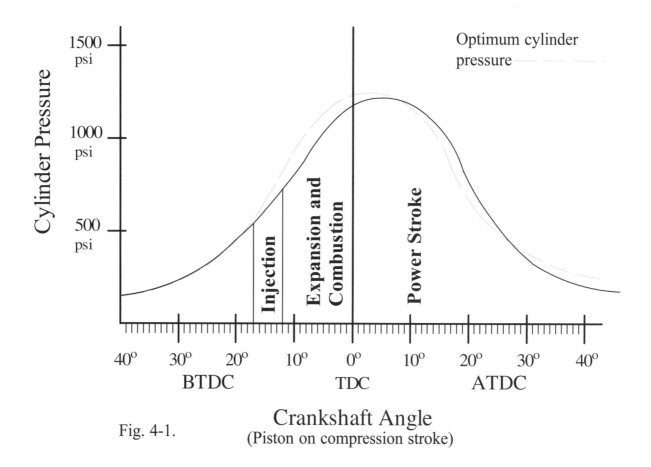

Fig. 4-1.

Crankshaft Angle
(Piston on compression stroke)

The pressure curve in Fig. 2-17, p. 18 shows start of injection at 20° BTDC and end of injection at 15° BTDC. A small amount of wear in the injection pump drive components can retard the timing a few degrees. Fig. 4-1 shows start of injection at 17° BTDC and end of injection at 12° BTDC. The fuel that is injected at 17° BTDC will have time to expand and burn completely, but the fuel injected at 13° BTDC will not.

Consequently, what you see with this condition is a little 'trailer' of white exhaust that is usually seen on acceleration. The engine could start well, run well, have good power and still have this little 'trailer' of white exhaust, and may also show some white exhaust at idle. The solution is to advance the static (pump-to-engine) timing slightly to compensate for this wear. Changing pump-to-engine timing should only be done after learning the timing procedure for your particular engine. Pump-to-engine timing should *never* be changed while the engine is running. Doing so can cause severe injury and also damage the engine and/or fuel system. All injection pumps and parts must be secured while the engine is running. Only make timing adjustments with the engine stopped. If advancing the timing slightly, 2-4 crankshaft degrees for example, clears up a little 'trailer' of white exhaust, then you can assume that the cause was normal wear of the injection pump and drive components. When troubleshooting this way, be sure to make marks of where the timing was originally set, so that it can be set back if the problem is not solved.

Comparing the two cylinder pressure curves in Fig. 4-1, you can see that the pressure curve representing retarded timing doesn't make as much cylinder pressure as the optimum pressure curve. The small loss of power from the timing being retarded by a few degrees may not be noticeable. However, the more the injection timing is retarded, the worse the loss of power, and the heavier the white exhaust.

Timing devices in fuel injection systems are generally very reliable components, but they do fail occasionally. A speed advance timing device failure would cause some white exhaust at higher engine RPMs or at all engine speeds. The start-of-injection timing would not advance as needed as the engine RPMs increased, and the injection timing would be retarded. Retarded injection timing doesn't allow the vaporized fuel the time necessary for complete combustion. After incomplete combustion, part of the vaporized fuel remains and becomes white-colored exhaust.

On some engines, injection pump drive components may break or slip, causing the timing to change suddenly. If the pump-to-engine timing 'slips time' a small amount, the result could be an engine that still runs, but suddenly starts making white exhaust, and could have some loss of power. The more the timing has 'slipped,' the worse the engine will run with heavier white exhaust, or not run at all. If a pump-to-engine timing change is suspected, the timing of the injection pump to the engine should be checked. Refer to your service manual for the timing procedure of your particular engine. If the pump-to-engine timing procedure for your engine requires flow timing, be sure to have all the proper tools, follow service manual procedures exactly, and be especially careful and clean when handling injection pump parts.

Another cause of white exhaust from a warmed-up engine is that the engine is worn and is not making the compression that it should. Although the injection timing hasn't changed, the process is slowed because the cylinder is not making compression and heat as fast as it should. Removing the oil filler cap while the engine is running and observing the white-colored crankcase vapors (blow-by) is a good indicator of the severity of compression loss.

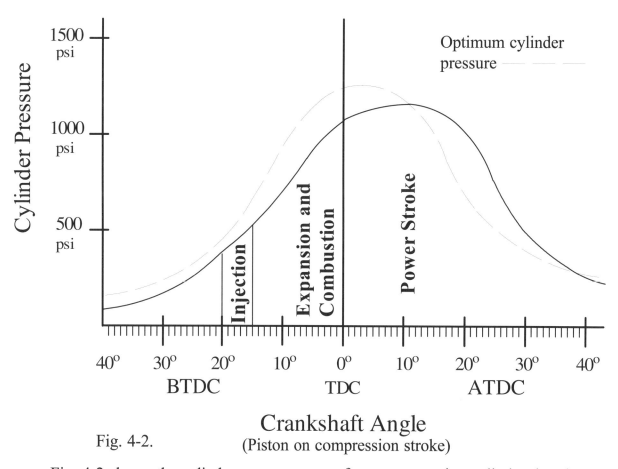

Fig. 4-2.

Crankshaft Angle
(Piston on compression stroke)

Fig. 4-2 shows the cylinder pressure curve for a worn engine cylinder that doesn't make full compression. At the time of injection, less oxygen and less heat is available for expansion and combustion, so the process is slowed. Expansion and some combustion occur, but not enough to burn all of the white fuel vapor. The worse the loss of compression, the slower the process becomes. Compared to the optimum cylinder pressure curve, you can see that the cylinder pressure produced from a worn engine makes less maximum cylinder pressure, which makes less power. As more compression is lost, the expansion and combustion process becomes slower, less power is generated, and more white exhaust is created.

Note that depending on the level of wear on the engine, ambient heat, and different engine designs and peculiarities, as a diesel engine wears and begins to lose compression, the exhaust can become black as well. This occurs when some compression is lost to decrease the amount of oxygen available for combustion, but not enough compression is lost to make the cylinder temperature fall below the 600° F needed for combustion. Essentially, we have an overfueling condition that causes black smoke. An engine in this condition of being partly worn out will produce more white exhaust when warming up, and can expel black exhaust when fully warmed up. As the engine wears and loses more compression, the black smoke turns to gray, and then to white when the engine is warmed up and working under load. A corresponding loss of power will occur as the engine wears and the exhaust turns from black to gray to white. When troubleshooting these problems, a compression test will help you prove or disprove the engine as the cause of the problem.

With this type of engine wear, we assume that all cylinders of the engine have worn out in essentially the same manner and that they are similarly low on compression. But you can also have a single cylinder that is low on compression while the other cylinders are in good shape. You could also have one cylinder causing all the white exhaust that you see. Usually you will hear a 'miss' or 'partial miss' depending on the severity of the compression loss. The cylinder causing the problem can be found by breaking loose (cracking) the injection line nuts at the injectors one at a time, looking at the exhaust, and listening to the response of the engine. Be sure to consult your service manual and observe all safety and environmental precautions. Although diesel fuel is not flammable like gasoline, it is combustible and could ignite if it lands on a hot exhaust system. Cracking an injection line nut is similar to pulling spark plug wires one at a time to check each cylinder on a gasoline engine. You are essentially 'shorting out' each cylinder of fuel one at a time. The cylinder that shows no change or less of a change in the running of the engine when 'shorted-out' is suspect. Re-tighten the injection line nut to the injector every time before loosening the next one. One cylinder may have lost compression for any number of reasons. The cylinder could have worn prematurely. An intake or exhaust valve could be leaking compression or stuck open. A head gasket could be blown. A hole or crack could have blown through the piston or cylinder wall. A compression washer may be missing from an injector, or the injector hold-down or glow plug may not be tight in the head, letting compression blow by.

An injector can cause white exhaust and engine 'miss' if the needle valve in the nozzle body breaks, sticks open from fuel contamination, or the nozzle itself breaks apart. Compression blows up through the injector into the injection line, and can go into the injection pump. The cylinder smokes white because the injection pump still manages to pump some fuel into the cylinder, but since there is lower compression and less heat, the fuel delivered to the cylinder turns to the white fuel vapor. Partial combustion may occur depending on the heat available, but a significant amount of white fuel vapor remains and is pushed out the exhaust. In such a case, the timing of injection is also affected because the force of compression has pushed the fuel back up into the injector. Any fuel that is injected will be late. Retarded injection timing in one cylinder adds to the engine 'miss' and white exhaust. This problem is easily found by 'shorting out' each injector one at a time.

Another way an injector can cause white exhaust is if the injector spring (see Fig. 2-32, p. 31) has broken, has worn, or has been incorrectly adjusted. If the opening pressure of the injector is lower than the maximum cylinder pressure from combustion, the pressure in the cylinder will overcome the spring in the injector, lift the needle valve off its seat and blow combustion into the injector and injection line. The loss of compression would again make this cylinder 'run cold,' blow some white exhaust, and depending on the severity of the compression loss, cause a 'miss,' a 'partial miss,' or a dead cylinder. Cracking each injection line, listening to the engine, and looking at the exhaust will quickly take you to the source of the problem.

Many diesel manuals suggest that the injectors should be tested first for any white exhaust problem. However, it has been my experience that timing and compression problems are the main cause of white exhaust. An injector with a leaky nozzle valve seat may cause white exhaust because fuel is dribbling into the cylinder at the wrong time. But an injector in such bad shape will cause black exhaust as well, if the engine makes sufficient heat. In general, when a diesel engine produces only white exhaust after the engine is warmed up, the cause will be related to the lack of heat available at the time of injection, or the timing of injection is retarded.

It is also possible for a defective thermostat to cause white exhaust. If a thermostat is stuck open and doesn't allow the engine to run at the proper temperature, the ambient heat in the cylinder may be insufficient. The engine is 'running cold' and not enough heat is available at the time of injection. The fuel is injected into the cylinder at the right time, the atomized fuel turns into the white fuel vapor and begins to burn, but not enough heat is available to produce complete combustion. The result is white exhaust that could be more prevalent at idle. All engines should have a gauge for coolant temperature. If you see that your diesel engine is running cold according to the coolant temperature gauge, and is making white exhaust, make sure that your coolant system is operating correctly first before suspecting a timing or compression problem.

White exhaust from a warmed-up engine can also occur because the injection pump is malfunctioning, or worn out. Many injection pumps have internal or external timing devices that advance or retard the injection timing depending on RPM, load, or other conditions. A malfunctioning timing device can cause retarded injection timing and thereby cause some white exhaust. To make sure that the injection pump is the problem, you must know that the pump is being supplied with sufficient fuel pressure with no air in the fuel supply. Stanadyne and Lucas-CAV distributor injection pump timing devices can be affected by a restriction in the return line coming off of the injection pump. A severe or complete return line restriction can also affect fuel metering and cause low power or cause the engine to stall. Thorough troubleshooting includes making sure that all return lines (fuel lines returning from the injection pump to the tank or filter head) are not restricted.

White exhaust at low idle

When a diesel engine is idling, just enough fuel is injected to create just enough power to keep the engine running. Consequently, an engine can cool down considerably when idling. Since heat is created by the compression and combustion process, less ambient heat is available in the cylinder from a cooled-down engine, which may cause some white exhaust. It is possible for an engine to start and run normally with clean exhaust, but then make some white exhaust after the engine has cooled while idling. Many injection systems are designed to advance the injection timing for low idle to compensate for this condition and to make the engine cylinders run hotter. The failure of a low idle advance device will cause white exhaust at idle. A common misconception is that overfueling causes white exhaust at low idle. Increasing fuel delivery at idle only increases engine RPM and does not cause white exhaust.

Many industrial engines are not designed to idle for more than a few minutes, so that when they do idle, it doesn't take long for the engine to cool down and make white exhaust. I have run into this white exhaust at low idle problem mostly when industrial engines have been installed in trucks or other vehicles. The key to identifying this particular condition is to notice the exhaust when the engine is hot and is first brought to idle. If the exhaust is clean at that time and starts turning white after a few minutes, then the engine has cooled down sufficiently to cause white exhaust or the low idle advance device (if equipped) has failed.

Other white exhaust at low idle situations are caused by timing and/or compression problems. With timing and/or compression problems, white exhaust at idle is usually accompanied with colored exhaust at other engine speeds and load conditions, as previously discussed in the 'Light to moderate white exhaust, normal power' section.

Moderate to heavy white exhaust with loss of power

I'm sure that you see the pattern by now. The worse the loss of compression and the worse the change of retarded timing, the worse the white exhaust and loss of power. Severely worn engines may still run, but the white exhaust released is irritating and causes more pollution. These engines should be retired or rebuilt, but be sure that your engine is worn out. A compression test will show you that. If you find that your engine's compression is within specifications, and the engine still runs with heavy white exhaust and low power, then you can be sure that the problem is timing related.

A peculiarity of prechamber engines (Fig. 3-4, p. 38) is that a prechamber engine usually can run with the pump-to-engine timing set anywhere. Injection pumps can be installed severely out of time and even backwards, or 180° out of time. A prechamber engine with the pump-to-engine timing backwards will be hard to start but can still run. Although the engine won't have much more power than what is required to keep itself running and will barrel out white exhaust, it can run. This is because injection occurs on the exhaust stroke and the piston then draws in air for the intake stroke with the atomized fuel remaining in the prechamber and combustion chamber. The atomized fuel remaining in the cylinder and prechamber will expand from the heat of compression while the piston is on the compression stroke.

The cylinder will actually be compressing an air/fuel mixture. The heat of compression causes the atomized fuel to expand, creating enough cylinder pressure to force the piston down and make the engine run. Remember that the expansion of atomized diesel fuel to the white fuel vapor can account for as much as 80% of the total cylinder pressure. Expansion only of the air/fuel mixture creates barely enough power to make an engine run. A prechamber engine that starts hard, runs with no power, and has heavy white exhaust may have an injection pump severely out of time. A direct injection engine with a severe timing problem will usually not run at all. It will belch out white exhaust while trying to start.

Timing problems that cause heavy white exhaust and low power can also be caused by a failure of the fuel injection pump or fuel supply system. A defective injection pump or one that has worn out could cause or contribute to a loss of power with white exhaust. You should first be sure that the fuel supply system is not affecting the fuel injection pump (see Chapter 5).

The important point to remember is this: if an engine is in good working condition and makes proper compression, the fuel supply and fuel returns are not restricted or allowing air in the system, and the injection pump is timed correctly to the engine, then a loss of power with heavy white exhaust problem will be caused by the injection pump.

These examples of white exhaust problems will guide you when troubleshooting. The rule of thumb is that white exhaust problems are caused by retarded timing, low compression, or a cold engine, with one major exception. Occasionally, gasoline is mistakenly used to fill a fuel tank for a diesel engine. The engine quickly begins to run rough, lose power or stall, expel a tremendous amount of white exhaust soon after fueling, and is difficult to restart. Having realized the mistake, only a professional should drain and flush the fuel supply and fuel injection systems. It is also possible that the gasoline introduced into the injection system will cause damage due to the lack of lubricity of gasoline. The close fitted hydraulic pumping parts may 'seize' or bind up in this situation. In this most unfortunate situation, the entire fuel system may need to be repaired or replaced.

Light to moderate black exhaust, normal power

We've established that atomized diesel fuel injected into the combustion chamber's hot compressed air will first vaporize into a white-colored fuel vapor, and the white fuel vapor is what burns. Besides heat, the white fuel vapor needs oxygen to burn. The oxygen is, of course, in the air, which is drawn through the air filter and into the combustion chamber. Under optimum conditions, there will be sufficient oxygen present to burn all of the fuel injected in the combustion chamber. Combustion occurs like an exploding firecracker. The mini-explosion burns all the fuel, creates the rest of the expansion to make the maximum cylinder pressure occur just after TDC and forces the piston down to make power for the engine. Even under optimum conditions, a small amount of residue, or soot, will be formed.

The most common cause of light to moderate black exhaust is when injectors are worn and are not atomizing fuel correctly. If the injector does not create a fine enough mist from the fuel, then the little droplets of fuel are too big and are not able to vaporize completely to a white fuel vapor. When the burning process begins, the outer layer of the unvaporized droplets tries to burn as well. Sufficient heat is still available to complete the burn process with the white fuel vapor, but the remaining droplets of fuel end up 'burnt' or 'cooked,' as the inside of the droplet of fuel is not exposed to any oxygen. The burnt droplets of fuel come out of the exhaust as very fine particles of black soot. The worse the injector atomizes the fuel, the worse the black exhaust becomes.

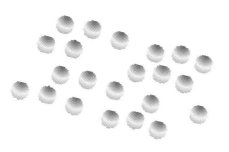

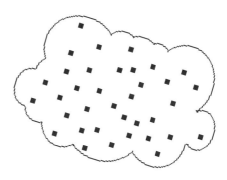

Fig. 4-3.

Magnified view of improperly atomized fuel.

Fig. 4-4.

Improperly atomized fuel contacts the engine cylinder's hot compressed air.

The longer an engine runs with worn injectors and a black exhaust problem, the more likely it becomes that another condition will arise. The excessive black soot will cling to areas of the combustion chamber and to the top of the piston. As this layer of soot builds up, the amount of space available to burn the fuel decreases. This can add significantly to a black smoke problem. Solving black exhaust problems usually requires removing the injectors for testing, service, or replacement, but not until the other causes are checked.

Light to moderate black exhaust with normal power can also be caused by an air restriction, such as a dirty air filter. Since less oxygen will be available to burn, not all of the white fuel vapor can react with oxygen and burn properly. The remaining vaporized fuel has sufficient heat but not enough oxygen. Since diesel fuel is an organic substance, overcooking or burning creates charred black particles. The worse the air restriction, the heavier the black smoke from the exhaust and the more likely it is that a loss of power will occur. Make sure that the air filter is in good condition.

A similar condition occurs when the injection pump delivers too much fuel, or overfuels. Again, we have a condition of sufficient heat and sufficient time to burn the fuel, but there is not enough oxygen in the combustion chamber to burn all of the fuel completely. A common misconception is that overfueling causes white exhaust. If everything is correct in the engine and fuel system, and the only thing wrong is that too much fuel is being injected into the cylinder, the result will be black exhaust, not white. The reasons for a fuel system delivering too much fuel are as numerous as the different types of systems. Advice from a fuel injection shop would be needed at this point for your particular system. As some types of fuel systems wear over several thousand miles or several hundred hours, they can gradually allow more fuel to be delivered. A black smoke problem caused by an overfueling injection pump will at least require the pump to be tested and calibrated, or will at most require the pump to be repaired or replaced.

Another cause of a black exhaust problem is when the pump-to-engine timing is too advanced. Let's go back to our graph of compression, injection, expansion, and combustion (see Fig. 2-17, p. 18). Start of injection occurs at 20° BTDC to completely burn the white fuel vapor and create optimum cylinder pressure. Figure 4-5 shows the pressure curve for the same engine cylinder except that the timing has been advanced and injection now starts at 26° BTDC.

If the pump-to-engine timing is advanced beyond specifications, the fuel is injected sooner than normal. The atomized fuel will still turn into a white fuel vapor and expand while it begins to burn, but the expansion and combustion occur too soon and the maximum cylinder pressure from combustion occurs while the piston is still BTDC; that is, the piston is still on its way up. One of the first things you will notice is that the engine runs louder. The piston has to fight against the pressure from expansion and combustion trying to force it back down until it gets past TDC. The engine essentially begins to fight itself.

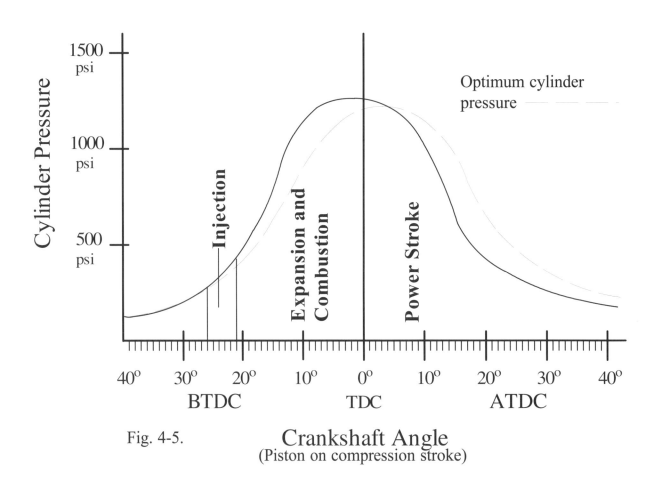

Fig. 4-5. Crankshaft Angle
(Piston on compression stroke)

As an engine continues to run with the timing too advanced, the combustion chamber gets hotter than normal because of the extra stress and load. Continuing to run the engine with the timing too advanced and the cylinders running too hot creates a surprising situation. The engine will have more power! It will also make black exhaust because some of the atomized fuel is being 'cooked' due to the excessive heat. But because the engine is running hotter, greater expansion occurs, and the engine creates more power. The drawbacks of running an engine this way to gain more power are that, in addition to making more pollution, the metals of the engine are not designed to run this hot for an extended period of time. Continued running of the engine with the timing too advanced will distort, crack, or break engine parts.

Pump-to-engine timing that is slightly too advanced may not make noticeable black exhaust, but the engine could be running a little too hot. This condition can occur after installing a new or rebuilt injection pump. Timing methods and procedures vary from engine to engine and some timing procedures are not as precise as others. If the engine runs louder with more combustion knock than normal after a pump installation, try retarding the pump-to-engine timing a few degrees with the engine stopped. Secure all parts and fasteners. After re-starting the engine and with the engine warmed up, if you see any white exhaust while the engine is working under load, stop the engine and return the pump-to-engine timing to its original setting. If you don't see any white exhaust, stop the engine and retard the pump-to-engine timing a few more degrees. Keep repeating this process, making sure that all parts and fasteners are secured before starting the engine, until you see some white exhaust while the engine is working under load. Then stop the engine and advance the timing a few degrees. With all parts and fasteners secured, start and run the engine. Working under load, the exhaust should be clean and the pump-to-engine timing will be set to its optimum point.

A severely worn or misadjusted timing device can advance the injection timing too fast and cause more 'knock' on acceleration, possibly with some black exhaust. The more the timing is advanced, the louder the engine will run.

There are a few other causes of a black smoke problem. You've already seen from the white exhaust sections that a small loss of compression may cause a black smoke problem. Now you can better understand why. Enough air was lost to cut down the amount of oxygen available to burn, but not enough compression was lost to decrease the heat necessary for combustion. Again, this is an overfueling situation.

Driving a diesel up a mountain road can cause an engine to make black exhaust. Beyond a 3000-foot elevation, the air becomes thin enough to affect the running of a diesel engine. At higher altitudes less oxygen is available from the same volume of air as at sea level, causing another overfueling condition. Some injection pumps are equipped with an altitude-sensing device that cuts back the maximum fuel available for injection as the altitude increases and atmospheric pressure decreases. However, other types of systems need to have the maximum fuel quantity decreased if an engine remains at higher altitudes.

If an exhaust gas recirculating (EGR) system is not working correctly, black exhaust could result. An EGR system recirculates exhaust gas to the intake manifold at idle and at the beginning of acceleration. This reduces the amount of oxygen present in the combustion chamber and thus reduces the formation of nitrogen oxides (NOx). Sufficient oxygen is still available for complete combustion at idle. Excessive NOx is created after an engine has been working under load and is brought down to idle. The ambient engine temperature is very hot. The extra heat and the excess oxygen in the cylinder allow the formation of excessive NOx. Therefore, reducing the amount of oxygen available at idle by recirculating exhaust gas to the intake manifold reduces the formation of NOx. After beginning to accelerate, the EGR valve should close and stop the flow of exhaust gas to the intake manifold.

If the EGR valve is malfunctioning or broken and does not close the flow of exhaust gas, the engine begins to smoke black while it is working because less oxygen is available to burn a full-load quantity of fuel. A by-product of an EGR system failure causing black exhaust is that the excessive soot will cling to the walls of the air intake channels and EGR passageways and eventually decrease the size of all EGR air flow channels. This can progress to the point that the channels become restricted and cannot feed the cylinder with enough air, consequently creating more of a black smoke problem. Continuing to run the engine this way will also cause a build-up of soot in the combustion chamber. Excessive soot build-up decreases the volume for expansion and combustion to occur, which increases compression and heat, and compounds a black smoke problem.

Quite often, black exhaust problems can be combination problems. An engine may have worn injectors, an air filter may need to be changed, and an uninformed person may have advanced the pump-to-engine timing to get more power. Continuing to run an engine this way, oblivious to the excessive exhaust, will not only create more pollution but will also severely decrease the life of the engine. Not until each problem is diagnosed and corrected will the engine run properly.

Moderate to heavy black exhaust, normal power

These problems are usually attributed to overfueling and/or worn injectors. Some people deliberately adjust the fuel systems to overfuel their engines to try and get more power. I highly recommend against doing this. This subject is discussed further in Chapter 7. While the power gained by overfueling is marginal, the engine wear and tear increases dramatically. As discussed earlier, severely worn injectors can cause black exhaust. The more wear on the injector, the more black exhaust will be created.

Moderate to heavy black exhaust, low power

This problem can be caused by a near complete restriction of the air supply. The engine has fuel and heat, but without oxygen the fuel won't vaporize properly and combustion won't occur correctly. The fuel will cook, burn, and come out black.

Another possible cause of moderate to heavy black exhaust and apparent low power is an engine that is overloaded. A good example is an industrial application such as a water pump. If the load applied to the engine surpasses the power capability of the engine, the engine begins to slow down, or bog down. The engine very quickly begins to run hotter because the expansion and explosion of combustion which forces the piston down is being opposed and overcome by the excessive load being applied to the engine. The engine is physically being forced to slow down while it is trying as hard as it can to keep running. With a hotter running engine, some of the atomized fuel doesn't burn correctly and 'cooks,' causing black exhaust.

Loss of power, light to moderate black exhaust

This particular problem is the same as the 'Loss of power, clean exhaust' problem discussed earlier, except that some black exhaust could be caused by worn injectors and/or a partially restricted air cleaner. This could be another combination problem for which all problems must be identified and handled separately. A linkage adjustment or a fuel filter service may be required to correct the loss of power. Change the air filter if it hasn't been done recently, and an injector service may be needed to solve the black smoke problem.

NOx, Particulates, and Hydrocarbons

NO_2 or NO are commonly referred to as NOx, or oxides of nitrogen. These are pollutants found in diesel exhaust. Excessive NOx and particulates, or soot (black exhaust) are one result of the pump-to-engine timing being too advanced. Advancing the timing increases particulates and NOx and decreases hydrocarbons (HC). Retarding the timing increases HC and decreases particulates and NOx. The optimum point of pump-to-engine timing is where these two graphs cross (see Fig. 4-6, p. 62). The pump-to-engine timing is critical. But even when the timing marks are lined up according to the service manual, or a timing meter shows the timing to be correct, also consider what the exhaust is telling you. Timing marks are always a good place to start, but they don't always mean that this is where the engine will run the cleanest. Quite often, when replacing or retiming an injection pump, you can have an engine that starts well, runs well, has good power, but has a little 'trailer' of white exhaust when warmed up and working. As in the 'Light to moderate white exhaust, normal power' section of this Chapter, if you can eliminate this 'trailer' of white exhaust by advancing the pump-to-engine timing slightly, then the system is in time. You would not advance the timing so much as to create black smoke or make the engine run too hot. But by advancing the timing just enough to make that white exhaust disappear, you give the white fuel vapor the time it needs to burn completely.

Of course, when making timing changes, make marks so that you can return timing to the original point if needed, and only make timing changes with the engine stopped. All engine and fuel system parts and fasteners must be secure while cranking or running. Always observe safety precautions and use common sense.

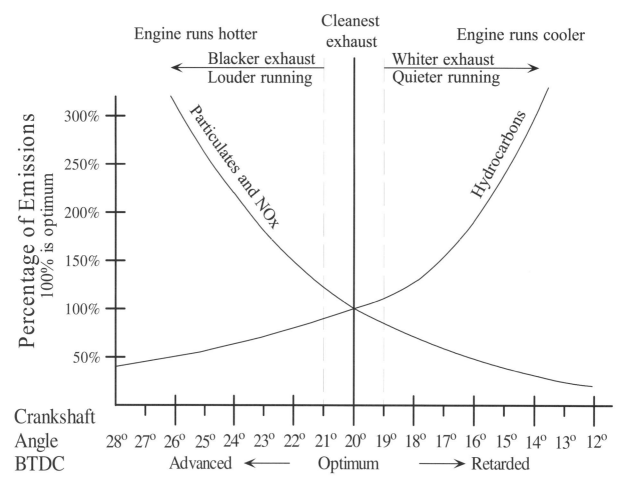

Fig. 4-6.   Start-of-injection timing
(Piston on compression stroke)

The graph in Fig. 4-6 is based on start-of-injection timing being optimum at 20°
BTDC as in the graph in Fig. 2-17, p. 18. The prechamber engine graph in Fig. 3-5, p. 39
would have an optimum start-of-injection timing of 35° BTDC. In general, optimum start-
of-injection timing has a tolerance of plus or minus one crankshaft degree. The area within
the dashed lines represents the optimum start-of-injection timing. Injection timing set to the
optimum point is critical for the engine to run clean and correctly. If you've identified the
cause of a white or black exhaust problem as being timing-related, you will be able to judge
the exhaust and engine sound to adjust the pump-to-engine timing properly to bring it back
into the optimum range, provided that any timing device(s) are functioning correctly.
Malfunctioning timing devices can cause colored exhaust and runability problems.

A properly timed engine and fuel injection system should run very clean under all
normal operating conditions. Allowing a diesel engine to run out-of-time not only causes
more pollution, but decreases the life expectancy of your engine and costs you money.

Black and white exhaust

It is possible for one engine cylinder problem to make white exhaust while another engine cylinder problem makes black exhaust. The exhaust may have a grayish color, but quite often you can distinctively see the black and white exhaust. If two injection lines are crossed and not installed to their correct pump outlet and corresponding injector, one cylinder will run with injection timing too advanced, and another will run with injection timing too retarded. The engine will run very rough with a significant amount of colored exhaust. Incorrect engine valve timing or valve leakage can cause black, gray, or white exhaust depending on the severity of the compression loss.

However, black and white exhaust situations are usually combination problems. Worn injectors, overfueling, or an air restriction making black exhaust with one engine cylinder low on compression, all cause black and white exhaust. Each problem must be identified and corrected. An engine in this kind of shape definitely needs some attention.

Other colored exhaust

Before concluding this Chapter, let's review the other colors of diesel exhaust and what they mean. Blue exhaust means that engine oil is burning. A bluish tint is common in the white exhaust from a timing or compression problem. In such conditions, a small amount of oil may be present with the white fuel vapor. A darker blue exhaust means that a significant amount of engine oil is burning. Oil can leak into the combustion chamber from a worn valve guide or a turbocharger, or can be pushed up on the cylinder walls by worn rings and cylinders.

By the time an engine is worn to the point that it is pushing up oil in the combustion chamber, the compression has dropped significantly and the engine is making excessive white exhaust. An engine with this level of wear should be retired or rebuilt. I make this point because continuing to run an engine in this condition can be dangerous. Besides causing excessive pollution, an engine worn to this point can push enough oil into the combustion chamber that the oil can begin to burn and create extra power. An engine can begin to 'run away' or accelerate uncontrollably, possibly causing damage or injury. When an engine does 'run away' by running on engine oil, the exhaust will be a heavy blue color. The engine will continue to run away until it runs out of oil to burn or something breaks, or the operator manages to apply enough load to slow down and stop the engine. A runaway engine can also be stopped by completely blocking the air supply. Please be aware that being close to a runaway engine is dangerous in itself. Engine parts could break at any time and cause severe injury. Even being close to the air intake is dangerous. An engine creates tremendous vacuum and can suck in anything close to it. It can be a scary situation, but it is totally avoidable.

The only other color of diesel exhaust that I have seen is brown. There is only one cause of brown exhaust -- dirty fuel. Brown exhaust, although not common, can be seen in marine applications. A fuel tank either on the boat, or at a storage facility, or at a fueling station will be corroded to the point that the bottom of the fuel tank is covered with a layer of brown, rusty sediment.

Marine applications continually move up and down in the water and tend to keep swirling and mixing the fuel. With fuel in this condition, even the best fuel filters can only do so much. The filtered fuel will still have a brown or rusty coloration, and will even stain your hands. When burned in the engine, the exhaust will have a brown color to it. This is definitely an extreme situation that deserves proper attention.

It should be noted that this analysis of diesel exhaust and the associated problems and causes apply to diesel engines with other fuel system types as well, such as Cummins or Detroit Diesel. White exhaust will still be caused by a timing or compression problem. Overfueling or injectors not spraying correctly will certainly cause black exhaust.

More than any part of this handbook, understanding this Chapter along with Chapter 3 will help you to understand your diesel engine and save money. We can draw several conclusions from this Chapter. The three ingredients needed for proper combustion are fuel, heat, and oxygen. Overfueling, excessive heat, or decreasing oxygen create black exhaust. Decreasing heat only makes white exhaust. Advancing the injection timing creates black exhaust. Retarding the injection timing creates white exhaust. Blue exhaust means that engine oil is burning, and brown exhaust means that your fuel tank or fuel supplier needs some attention.

You've read about several runability problems that are caused by defects that are not in the fuel injection system. The bottom line is that you want to eliminate all possibilities before removing an injection pump or injector for repair or replacement.

When problems arise, this exhaust analysis can put you on the right track and on the road to remedy.

Chapter 5 - Diesel Fuel and Fuel Supply Systems

Diesel fuel quality

The longevity of a diesel fuel injection system is dependent on fuel quality, fuel filtration, and water separation. First, what is good quality fuel? Since the United States and many other countries have acted to make refineries produce low sulfur diesel fuel, fuel quality has improved in some ways and has become worse in others. The cetane number rates the ignition quality of a diesel fuel. The higher the cetane number, the easier the fuel can be ignited. Cetane rating is more consistent from one refinery to another than in the past. The changes in the chemical composition of the fuel reduce the formation of pollutants containing sulfur. However, the process needed to produce low sulfur diesel decreases the lubricity of the fuel and causes fuel system parts to wear faster. Internationally, diesel fuel can range from exceptionally well-refined to the poorest-quality fuel. Generally, the higher quality diesel fuel will cost a little more per gallon. High-quality diesel fuel is clear or has a light amber tint. Some diesel fuel supplies are dyed a red, blue, or green color to identify the fuel for sulfur content or for tax purposes by the government.

Diesel fuel is labeled as number-one or number-two. Number-one diesel fuel is used in cold weather and has a lower viscosity (pourability) than number-two diesel. The lighter number-one fuel is more stable in cold weather, as it has a lower gel point. Gel point is the temperature at which diesel fuel starts to become solid. Since number-one diesel fuel is thinner than number-two diesel fuel, fuel injection components are supplied with even less lubrication and wear out faster. Jet fuel is basically diesel fuel with a lower viscosity than number-one diesel. Although jet fuel and number-one diesel fuel are almost indistinguishable, using jet fuel in a diesel fuel injection system will cause pumping unit seizure. The thinner jet fuel does not supply the lubricity needed for the hydraulic pumping units.

Low quality fuel can cause low power, white or black exhaust, and premature wear or failure of a fuel injection system. Diesel fuel with a lower cetane number can cause lower power and some colored exhaust. Some people have little or no choice of where they buy fuel. But if you do have a choice, find a fuel outlet that sells a lot of fuel. Also, avoid fuel that has been in storage for a long time. Diesel fuel can deteriorate over time and can quickly cause a fuel injection system to malfunction. If fuel must be stored, make sure that it is not exposed to the elements. When buying fuel, it is preferable to have the fuel dispensed through a water separator and fuel filter. Because this is not always possible, it is vital that your diesel engine be equipped with proper fuel filtration plus a water separator.

Poor quality diesel fuel, improper water separation, and improper filtering are the three most likely causes of an early fuel system failure. Spending a few pennies more per gallon for the best fuel available, or being careful and asking questions about fuel quality from the refinery or fuel station, is time and money well spent. Just having your engine equipped with a water separator and fuel filter is not enough. Even when using good quality fuel, water separators must be checked and drained regularly and fuel filters must be replaced from time to time. Usually diesel engines are equipped from the factory with sufficient filtration and water separation systems, but sometimes they are not.

Water separation

A common misconception is that a fuel filter will remove or filter out water. Water will pass through a fuel filter as easily as water passes through a swimming pool filter. Since water is heavier than diesel fuel, it will fall to the bottom of the filter canister or pass through the filter with the turbulence of the moving fuel. Having a water separator for your diesel engine should be mandatory. Of equal importance is being able to detect water that has collected in the separator and to be able to drain the water. Some water separators have no means of water detection other than by draining some fuel to see if any water is present. This type of system presupposes that the operator will open the drain every day and check for water, and that the amount of water possibly traveling through the system will be no greater than the capacity of the water separator itself. If a water separator fills with water and is not drained, when more water comes through, the water will not be separated and will pass right through the filters and into the fuel injection system. Water separators must be constantly maintained. Once water gets into a fuel injection system, it can oxidize and form rust or other corrosive solids on the internal fuel system parts. It doesn't take much water to affect the close fitted, fast moving pumping parts or other fuel system parts and cause premature failure. Water contamination of an injection pump and/or injectors is costly and unnecessary.

I always recommend a water separator with a clear bowl so you can easily see the water and drain it out. Use a drip pan or some other receptacle to collect the water and diesel fuel being drained from a water separator and dispose of it properly. Some separators can be purchased with a water-sensing kit that lights an indicator when the water in the separator has reached a certain level. Most water separators include a fuel filter, as well.

Water can get into your fuel in several ways. You can get water in your fuel at the fuel station. In areas where the temperature gets hot during the day and cold at night, condensation can form on the walls of your fuel tank and run down into the fuel. Keeping your tank full is good prevention against condensation. If a storage tank is outside and exposed to the elements, make sure that no rain or runoff can enter the tank. Above-ground fuel storage tanks usually have water drains on the bottom of the tanks which should also be checked regularly.

In many types of equipment, the fuel tank has a water drain on the bottom of the tank and should be opened and drained regularly. Again, it is preferable to fill your engine's fuel tank with fuel that has already been run through a water separator and filter. You should make every effort not to get water in your tank in the first place. Moreover, the water separator for your engine must be checked regularly or even daily or hourly depending on your fuel source and usage. It doesn't take a great volume of water to form some rust or corrosion in the injection system and cause it to fail. This little bit of prevention can save you hundreds of dollars in repair costs.

A water separator is really a simple device. Fuel enters through one side and since water is heavier than diesel fuel, the water will fall to the bottom of the separator. Water separators usually have fuel filters incorporated into the units. The water-separated fuel is filtered and moves on to the next stage in the fuel supply.

Fig. 5-1.
Cut-away view of a Racor
water separator and fuel filter.

1 Feed tube
2 Fuel filter
3 Fuel inlet
4 Fuel outlet
5 Clear polymer bowl
6 Water
7 Water drain

 Fuel flow

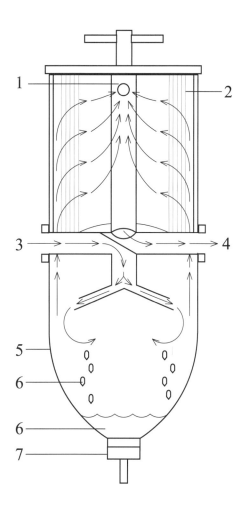

Fuel filters

Fuel filters are as important as water separators. The diesel fuel itself lubricates the hydraulic injection components and other moving parts. Fuel that is not free of water and not perfectly clean will cause the pumping parts to wear or fail prematurely. Larger engines that use a great deal of fuel have two or more fuel filters. The first filter may be rated 20 micron, meaning that the smallest particles that can pass though are no larger than 20 micron. A micron is one one-thousandth of a millimeter (0.001 mm). The next filter will have a smaller rating such as 5 or 10 micron. Unless specified by the manufacturer, the final stage fuel filter should be 2-micron. Many smaller diesel engines use only a single 2 micron filter. Any particles that pass through a 2-micron filter will not cause significant or premature wear to the fuel system. Fuel filters/water separators can always be added or changed to accommodate higher fuel usage or severe conditions. Fuel filter cartridges should be changed regularly and extra cartridges kept with your vehicle or machine.

Fuel additives

Supplying your fuel injection system with perfectly clean fuel that is free of water is the best situation. However, most fuel that we use now is a low sulfur version. The processes used to refine this variety of fuel to make the fuel lower in sulfur also lowers the fuel lubricity. Since the diesel fuel is the only lubrication for the hydraulic pumping parts, and for some injection pump types the only lubrication for the entire pump, this variety of 'dry diesel' fuel tends to wear out fuel system parts faster than before the change to low sulfur fuel. The solution is to use a good fuel additive.

Many fuel additives for diesel fuel do more harm than good. Alcohol-based or water-dispersing additives are the main culprits. Combining two or more different types of additives can cause chemicals to react and form corrosive solids on the pumping parts, causing premature failure. If you buy good quality fuel, filter it properly and keep it free of water, then there are only a few additives that you will ever need.

Stanadyne Performance Formula fuel additive will restore the lubricity lost through refining without causing more pollution. This additive has other qualities as well, such as lowering the gel point in cold weather, a cetane enhancer for a little more power and better fuel economy, and corrosion and buildup inhibitors to keep the fuel system parts clean. This additive is made by a fuel system manufacturer and has been proven to do the job. I'm not saying that this is the only additive that works. But in my experience, I have seen countless fuel system failures caused by fuel additives. If you use a particular fuel additive that you are satisfied with, keep using it. If you aren't sure or do not use fuel additives at all, then Stanadyne Performance Formula additive should be used with every fill-up.

Stanadyne Performance Formula fuel additive is especially needed in cold weather applications and with number-one diesel fuel, which has even fewer lubricating properties than number-two diesel. Stanadyne also sells a cold weather additive for extra insurance in cold weather. The money you pay for the additive is money in the bank, as your fuel system will last longer and your engine will run better. Fuel injection shops, repair shops, and some service stations carry these products, as well as fuel filters and water separators.

Many people have to store their own fuel, or use fuel that has been stored for extended periods of time. Be aware that while fuel additives designed to slow down fuel deterioration accomplish their task, the strong chemicals in fuel storage additives can shorten the life of your fuel injection system. Any fuel additive should be used only as directed. In my opinion, if stored and treated fuel is the only fuel available, Stanadyne Performance Formula is the only other fuel additive that should be used.

Diesel fuel in a stored engine can deteriorate and solidify in the hydraulic pumping parts of the injection pump. It is preferable to start and run stored engines occasionally.

The other additive a diesel system may need is a biocide for bacteria or algae growth in the fuel tank and fuel supply system. Bacteria growth usually occurs in marine applications where the fuel is exposed to more moisture. Since diesel fuel can hold a small amount of water in stasis, and a fuel tank can easily have an amount of water at the bottom of the tank, a growth can begin and spread through the tank and into the fuel lines, fuel pumps, fuel filters, and injection pump. It doesn't take long before the fuel flow is restricted to the point that the injection pump can't pump and the engine will not run. Several brands of biocide are available. Some marine operators add small amounts of this additive on a regular basis for preventative maintenance. Algae growth in diesel fuel is most likely caused by fuel storage tanks that have this growth already present. Again, be particular about the fuel you buy when you can. While this growth problem is most likely to be seen in boats, algae growth problems can occur in any diesel application. If you have a water separator with a clear plastic bowl, you will see the algae growth on the sides of the clear bowl. If present, immediate treatment is necessary until the growth is gone.

This is the recipe for keeping your diesel fuel injection system maintained and working properly throughout its service life. Buy good quality fuel which is already filtered and water separated, keep your fuel tanks full if possible, and check and maintain your fuel filters and water separator systems regularly. Use Stanadyne Performance Formula additive with every fill-up. Use a biocide for bacteria growth only if needed or as preventative maintenance for marine applications.

Fuel supply systems

Besides supplying clean fuel to the injection system, the fuel needs to be supplied under low pressure to the injection system. Keep in mind that a fuel supply system may have to move a large volume of fuel, but only a small amount of that fuel is used for injection. The rest of the fuel is used to lubricate and cool the injection system and is then returned to the fuel tank or filter head by means of a return line. Depending on the design of the fuel injection system, restriction of a fuel return line may cause a loss of power or may cause the engine to stall. All fuel supply and return lines must be in good condition and unrestricted.

Let's look at different configurations of fuel supply systems and how certain failures can cause the fuel injection system to malfunction.

Pumps that transfer fuel from the tank to the fuel injection system are called fuel pumps, supply pumps, lift pumps, or transfer pumps. They all accomplish the same task and, for the sake of simplicity, they will be called supply pumps.

The simplest supply system is a gravity-feed system, in which the fuel tank is higher than the injection pump.

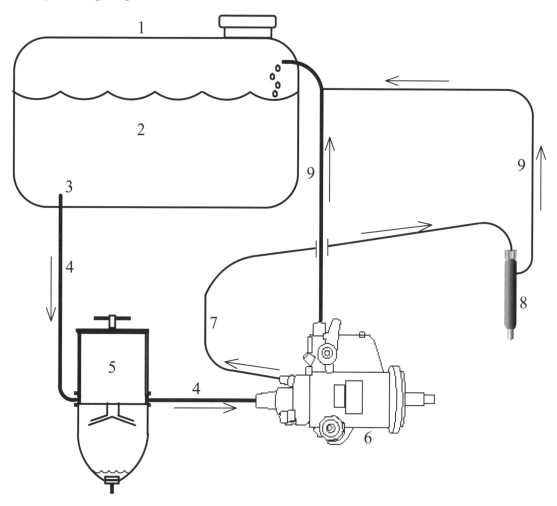

Fig. 5-2.
Gravity-feed fuel supply system.

1 Fuel tank
2 Diesel fuel
3 Pick-up tube
4 Supply line
5 Fuel filter/water separator

6 Injection pump
7 Injection line
8 Injector
9 Return line

In Fig. 5-2, gravity forces the fuel down through the water separator and fuel filter to the injection pump. This simple system is generally trouble-free as long as the water separator and fuel filters are maintained and nothing enters the tank to plug the pick-up tube. The fuel return lines must be unrestricted.

On smaller engines, I have seen fuel supply systems with no supply pump and which are not gravity fed. This makes the injection pump pull the fuel all the way from the tank.

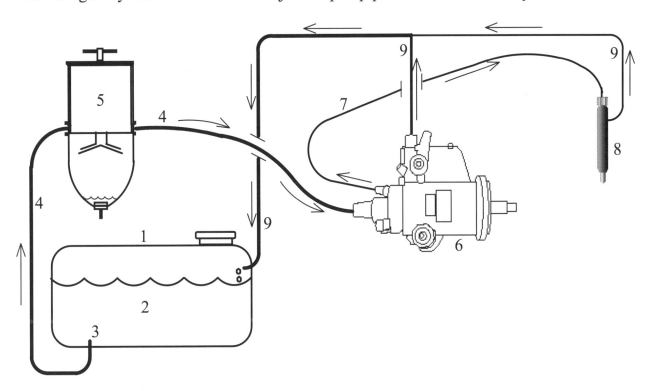

Fig. 5-3.
Injection pump suction fuel supply system.

1 Fuel tank	6 Injection pump
2 Diesel fuel	7 Injection line
3 Pick-up tube	8 Injector
4 Supply line	9 Return line
5 Fuel filter/water separator	

The inherent problem with this design is the creation of a vacuum in the fuel supply. Any defect in the system from the tank to the injection pump inlet will pull air into the fuel supply. Air bubbles in the fuel supply can make an engine run rough constantly or intermittently with a loss of power, surge, run and stall, not run at all, or be difficult to restart. As long as this type of fuel supply system is maintained, it can perform normally. However, the long run of vacuum simply makes this type of setup prone to problems.

It is preferable to have a small 5-psi supply pump pulling fuel from the tank and pushing the fuel to the injection system as in Fig. 5-4. In this way, the system is supplied with a positive flow of fuel and the injection pump does not have to draw the fuel in by itself.

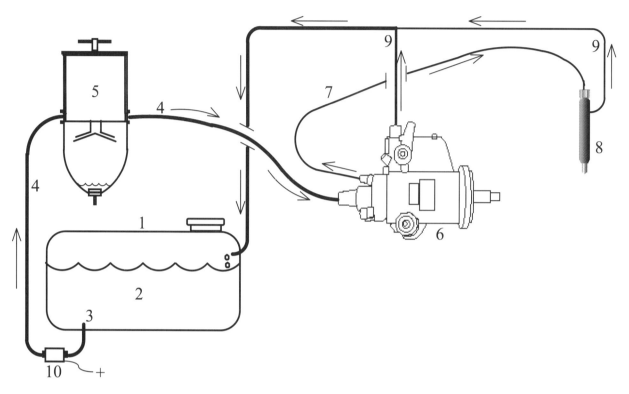

Fig. 5-4.
Supply pump pressurized fuel supply system.

1 Fuel tank	6 Injection pump
2 Diesel fuel	7 Injection line
3 Pick-up tube	8 Injector
4 Supply line	9 Return line
5 Fuel filter/water separator	10 Supply pump

If a fuel supply system is converted from a suction system, as in Fig. 5-3, to a pressurized system, as in Fig. 5-4, the fuel filter element type may need to be changed as well. Some fuel filters are designed to work in a pressurized environment, while others are designed to work in a vacuum environment. The proper 'suction side' or 'pressure side' fuel filter must be used. Otherwise, premature filter failure will result, causing a fuel restriction.

The fuel supply system in Fig. 5-4 is the most common. This fuel supply system uses a small supply pump that transfers fuel from the tank to the injection system. Some systems are set up so that the water separator is first in line before the supply pump. Other systems place all water separators and filters after the supply pump.

I prefer having all water separators and fuel filters on the pressure side of the supply pump because pulling fuel through a filter or water separator on the suction side of the supply pump causes a vacuum flow and again, is prone to pulling air into the fuel supply. Priming the system after changing filters is easier if the water separators and fuel filters are on the pressure side of the supply pump. Newer fuel filters and water separators incorporate a hand primer into the filter or water separator units to aid in priming the fuel supply system after changing the fuel filters. Other systems incorporate a hand primer into the fuel supply pump.

Some fuel supply systems are built with a supply pump inside the fuel tank. I like this version also because the fuel supply from the tank to the injection system is pressurized and air cannot be pulled into the system unless the engine has run out of fuel. Never allow a diesel engine to run out of fuel. Repriming the fuel supply after running a diesel out of fuel is time-consuming and can add wear and tear to starters and batteries. Keeping enough fuel in the tank is just common sense. Some diesel fuel supply systems have a filter screen or strainer in the fuel tank to prevent large particles from passing through to the fuel filters. I find this setup problematic, as the strainer can collect enough debris to cause a fuel restriction. In such a case, the tank must be removed and the strainer must be cleaned or removed.

Overflow valves and screws

A supply pump must move a certain volume of fuel. To create charge pressure in an inline injection pump fuel gallery, the supply pump flow must be partially restricted. Most inline injection pumps have a device called an overflow valve or overflow screw (see Fig. 2-2, p. 11). This part is normally in the shape of a bolt with a plunger and spring or an orifice built inside to create a regulated restriction.

Fig. 5-5.
Cut-away view of plunger and spring overflow valve.

1 Fuel flow from supply pump
2 Return fuel
3 Plunger
4 Spring
5 Spill port

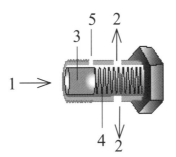

The fuel flow inside the inline injection pump fuel gallery pushes against the overflow valve plunger. Fuel is able to move between the plunger and the hollow screw body, creating a restriction which creates fuel pressure. The fuel pressure pushes against the plunger and compresses the spring. When the plunger moves far enough, the spill port is uncovered and fuel pressure is maintained at its designed level.

Fig. 5-6.
Cut-away view of orifice type overflow screw.

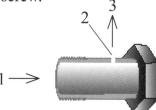

1 Fuel flow from supply pump
2 Orifice restrictor
3 Return fuel

The fuel flow inside an inline injection pump fuel gallery pushes into the hollow screw and through the orifice restrictor, which creates fuel pressure. Many orifice-type overflow screws have a filter screen built inside the hollow screw to prevent particles from clogging the orifice.

A small fuel restriction is necessary to allow the supply pump to create pressure and positive fuel flow to 'charge' the P&Bs (see Figs. 2-2, p. 11 and 2-4, p. 13). The overflow valve or screw creates a regulated restriction, allows small amounts of air to purge out of the injection pump fuel gallery while the engine is running, and provides cooling to the fuel injection system by carrying away heat in the return fuel. Usually, a large volume of fuel is returned through the overflow valve/screw and to the tank. Overflow valves/screws create restriction to develop pressures in the 5-30 psi range. Failure or malfunction of a plunger and spring overflow valve can cause low power usually with clean exhaust, but sometimes with white exhaust. Quite often the overflow valve spring breaks or the plunger sticks past the spill port so that sufficient supply pump pressure cannot develop. If the overflow valve doesn't create enough restriction, sufficient gallery pressure will not develop, and the pumping units will not receive a full 'charge' of fuel. The fuel metering will be affected, hence affecting the power output of the engine.

The overflow valve is usually the last bleeding point of the fuel supply. Most inline injection pumps are equipped with a plunger and spring overflow valve or an orifice-type overflow screw. Some inline injection pump types don't have an overflow valve, but have bleeder screws for the fuel gallery. Overflow valves are critical to the proper operation of an inline injection pump and to the proper operation of an engine. Removing an overflow valve for inspection or replacement is recommended when troubleshooting a low power or rough running problem on an engine equipped with an inline injection pump.

Fuel supply system failure

Many inline fuel injection pumps incorporate supply pumps as part of the unit. The fuel supply lines can be routed the same as with a separate supply pump. Remember that between the tank and the supply pump, called the 'suction side,' the supply pump is pulling fuel and creating a vacuum. Between these two points is where air can be drawn into the fuel supply.

Some supply pumps can also take in air when they fail. Since the supply pump pushes fuel through the fuel filter(s) and into the injection pump, any point after the supply pump is called the 'pressure side.' On the pressure side, any defect in the fuel supply system will leak and be easily seen.

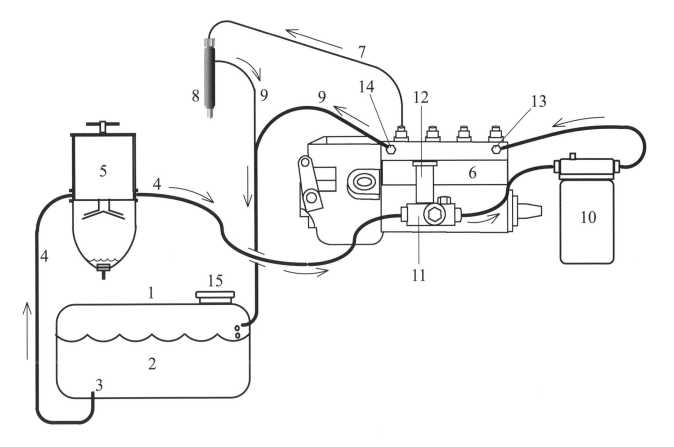

Fig. 5-7. Supply pump pressurized fuel supply system with inline injection pump.

1 Fuel tank	6 Injection pump	11 Supply pump
2 Diesel fuel	7 Injection line	12 Hand primer
3 Pick-up tube	8 Injector	13 Inlet screw
4 Supply line	9 Return line	14 Overflow valve (screw)
5 Fuel filter/water separator	10 Final stage fuel filter	15 Self-venting tank cap

Fig. 5-7 illustrates a common fuel supply system with the supply pump incorporated into an inline injection pump. Fuel flows from the tank to the supply pump under suction or vacuum. In this example, the water separator is on the suction side of the fuel supply pump. Fuel flows under pressure from the supply pump to the final stage filter, and to the injection pump. The overflow valve creates a regulated restriction against the supply pump fuel flow to create sufficient pressure to charge the P&Bs (see Figs. 2-2, p. 11 and 2-4, p. 13).

The fuel tank cap (see Fig. 5-7, position 15, p. 75) is an important part of the fuel supply system that is not normally considered as a possible cause of an engine runability problem. The tank cap is designed to vent so that excessive pressure or vacuum does not develop in the fuel tank. Since fuel is gradually being removed from the tank while the engine is running, a fuel tank cap that is full of dirt or has failed and cannot vent will cause the fuel tank to build up excessive vacuum. Excessive vacuum in the fuel tank can affect the fuel supply pressure to the fuel injection system and cause a loss of power, the same as with a fuel supply restriction. Slowly remove the tank cap and listen for a hissing sound. If you hear a large equalization occur, put the engine under load and see if the power and exhaust has improved. I have seen a few fuel tank caps not venting cause a loss of power problem. Dirt and mud were always the culprits. Although the fuel tank cap not venting is an uncommon problem, when eliminating all possible causes of a runability problem, removing the tank cap is standard procedure.

Fuel supply systems can fail for numerous reasons and cause the engine to run poorly or not at all. These failures can be sorted into fuel restriction problems and air ingress problems.

If your fuel filter becomes filled with sediment and does not allow enough fuel to pass, it will begin to restrict, or starve, the fuel supply of the injection system. Depending on the injection system, this problem can manifest itself by a loss of power, possibly with white exhaust. As the restriction becomes worse, the power loss can increase to the point that the system cannot supply enough fuel to keep the engine running. Changing fuel filters regularly will avoid this problem. Fuel restrictions can occur if a fuel supply line becomes plugged or kinked, or if something in the fuel tank is covering the pick-up tube. Starting from the tank, fuel flow can be checked one section at a time to eliminate possibilities and find the cause. A supply pump malfunction or failure will cause the same symptoms as a fuel restriction. Fuel restriction problems are usually easy to find and fix. Air ingress problems can be tougher to find and solve.

You've already learned that the only place a fuel supply system can pick up air is from the suction side of the supply pump, or from the supply pump itself. The problem of air bubbles in the fuel supply can manifest itself by causing the engine to run rough constantly or intermittently, lose power, surge, run and stall, be difficult to restart, or not start at all. Troubleshooting this problem begins with confirming the problem by checking the fuel supply going into or out of the injection pump, or by installing a clear hose on the injection pump supply line or return line. Sometimes, slightly breaking loose the injection pump inlet line and seeing bubbles or foam can confirm the presence of air. This cannot be done on fuel supply systems that have the injection pump pulling fuel from the tank (see Fig. 5-3 p. 71) because the entire fuel supply line is under vacuum. On some systems, air bubbles can be seen from the return line coming out of the injection pump by using a see-through fuel hose. Once an injection pump is primed, no dead air spaces exist inside the injection pump fuel gallery. If air goes into the injection pump, air bubbles or foam will be seen coming out of the injection pump return line. Be careful not to confuse fuel turbulence with air ingress when looking at return fuel. Some injection pumps require a large volume of fuel and return most of the fuel to the tank. The diesel fuel coming out of the injection pump return, or overflow, can be stirred up and appear to have air in it.

After you have verified the presence of air in the fuel, and knowing that air can only be picked up in the fuel supply on the suction side of the supply pump while the engine is running, you've narrowed the job down to a small area. Usually a fitting or hose clamp isn't quite tight enough or a hose has cracked, allowing air to be pulled into the fuel supply. Any filters, water separators, hand primers, tank switching devices, etc., on the suction side of the supply pump are suspect.

In especially difficult cases of fuel restriction or air ingress problems, it may become necessary to bypass the entire fuel supply system and run the fuel supply from a separate source to verify the problem. This is a common troubleshooting method. Be sure to observe all safety precautions and be sure that the diesel fuel being used is clean, filtered, and free of water.

After correcting a defect in a fuel supply system, or when changing fuel filters, the fuel supply system must be bled of air. Basically, you want to move fuel from the tank through the fuel supply system to the injection pump inlet while bleeding out any air. Some injection pumps require the fuel gallery or injection pump housing to be bled of air. Bleeding is accomplished in numerous ways. With the variety of parts, designs, and accessories, the engine or vehicle service manual should be consulted for correct bleeding procedures. Be careful not to burn up your starter if you experience a difficult priming or starting problem.

In a pump/line/injector system, after the fuel gallery or injection pump housing has been bled of air, the injection pump must be primed to the injectors. Priming the injection lines is accomplished by cracking the injection line nuts at the injectors and cranking the engine until fuel squirts from the injection line. Any shut-off device or shut-off lever must be set to run while priming the injection lines. The engine cannot start with all the injection line nuts cracked loose, because injection pressure cannot develop.

Fuel supply systems play a critical part in the proper running of a diesel engine. The designs and variations are numerous. A great number of unnecessary repairs are made because a fuel supply problem is not considered while troubleshooting. Fuel systems with a supply pump must create a certain amount of pressure and volume to feed the injection system. When troubleshooting any runability problems, you must know that your fuel supply system is supplying good quality, water-free, filtered fuel without any restriction or air to the fuel injection system and that all return lines are unrestricted.

Chapter 6 - Starting and Stalling Problems

When a diesel engine stalls or doesn't start, it is common to assume that something is wrong with the injection pump. Sometimes that is the case, but before removing any component for repair or replacement, proper troubleshooting is necessary because other problems can cause an engine to stall or not start. Unless otherwise noted, the engines in these examples are in good condition with a primed fuel system ready to deliver fuel as soon as the engine begins to turn. The starter must turn the engine fast enough, and in the correct rotation, to make sufficient compression and heat for expansion and combustion to occur. A low battery or a bad starter that doesn't turn the engine fast enough can cause a hard starting or no starting problem. Prechamber engines have glow plug systems to heat the prechamber to aid in starting. Many direct injection and prechamber engines have starting aids built into the injection pump, or have other external starting aids. For an engine to start, oxygen and heat are needed and a sufficient quantity of fuel must be injected at the right time.

Hard starting or no starting, very little or no exhaust

Very little or no exhaust indicates that little or no fuel is being injected into the cylinder. If the starter is turning the engine fast enough, the first items to check are: voltage supply to the solenoid(s); whether shut-off levers are fully open; whether fuel is available to the injection system; and whether air is in the fuel supply. If the injection system has sufficient fuel supplied to it, has its shut-off device open or energized correctly, but doesn't pump fuel when trying to start, the injection pump or the shut-off device probably has failed.

Only if an air-in-fuel problem is already present can enough air get into the injection pump, cause an 'air lock,' and prevent the injection pump from pumping even though fuel supply is sufficient. Some pump designs are more prone to 'air lock' than others. Some fuel injection pumps can be stubborn to prime after air has gone through them, especially on smaller engines. Repriming the injection pump involves first correcting any air or restriction problem in the fuel supply system. Next, you must be able to supply the injection pump with a positive flow of fuel with no air in the fuel. After the fuel supply is bled of air, you can crack, or break loose the injection line nuts at the injectors. If you know that the shut-off device is energized or the shut-off lever is set to run, you can then begin to crank the engine.

While cranking the engine, the cracked injection line allows any air in the injection line to be expelled and primes the injection pump to the injectors. Be sure to consult your engine service manual for proper procedure and safety precautions. At this point, if you are unable to see any fuel coming out of the injection line, then you can conclude that the injection pump is probably malfunctioning. On a few occasions, I have had to remove the injectors or glow plugs from an engine to allow the engine to turn at cranking speed without working against compression. This allows the engine and the injection pump to turn faster than usual and, in this way, I was able to get an 'air locked' injection pump to begin pumping again. A primed injection system will squirt a small amount of fuel under low pressure with the injection lines cracked or disconnected from the injectors. With an open system, the high fuel injection pressure cannot develop. If each cracked injection line nut leaks or squirts fuel without any air bubbles while cranking, tighten the line nuts, try to start the engine, and look at the exhaust.

Sometimes after a diesel engine sits overnight or longer and you try to start it, it may start and stall a few times, and then start and continue running, running rough occasionally, until the engine warms up. One may think that the engine is getting worn, or that the fuel injection system is malfunctioning, but what really could be happening is that the fuel supply to the injection pump has bled back. For this situation to occur, the fuel tank must be lower than the injection pump. Gravity-fed fuel supply systems do not have bleed-back problems if the tank is always higher than the injection pump. It is possible for a fuel supply system to bleed back only when the vehicle or equipment is kept on an incline, such as on a driveway. When kept on an incline, the tank could be lower than the injection pump and be prone to a bleed-back problem. In such a case, the fuel tank will be level with the injection pump when the vehicle or equipment is on flat ground.

Any defect in the fuel supply lines, fuel filters, water separators, etc., will let the fuel drain, or bleed back to the level of the fuel in the tank. If the defect is on the pressure side of the supply pump, you should see a fuel leak at the location of the defect while the engine is running. If the injection pump itself has a small fuel leak while running, it could cause the fuel to bleed back when not working. With the fuel bled back after sitting overnight, the first thing that happens is the engine starts and begins to run until the air in the supply line reaches the injection pump. The injection pump stops pumping fuel and the engine stumbles or stalls. At this point, the engine can be difficult to restart until the air has passed through the system. The remedy is to make sure that all fuel lines, hoses, filters, etc., are in good condition and are secured. Some types of injection pump and fuel supply systems can be prone to bleeding back by their own design. In such cases, low restriction, one-way valves are available to install in the fuel supply line that will stop the fuel from bleeding back.

Part of the fuel supply can be higher than the tank and be on the suction side of the supply pump, such as a water separator or fuel filter. A small defect in this area, such as a small crack in a fuel hose or a loose fitting, could cause the fuel to bleed back while not running (see Fig 5-7, position 5, p. 75). A defect like this, higher than the fuel tank and on the suction side, probably won't leak and will be difficult to find.

Upon starting the engine, the air that entered the fuel supply from the small bleed back makes its way to the injection pump and causes the engine to run rough and/or stall. If the defect is on the suction side, air will enter the fuel supply while the engine is running. Bleed-back problems can be diagnosed by the same method discussed in the 'Fuel supply system failure' section in Chapter 5.

One or more worn or defective injectors may cause an uncommon hard-starting problem. When a diesel engine is shut down, one of the pistons will be on the compression stroke and will make compression before stopping. With the engine stopped, the pressure in one cylinder will eventually bleed past the piston rings and into the crankcase. If the nozzle valve seat in an injector (see Fig. 2-32, position 12, p. 31) is leaking, and if the engine stops with the piston on the compression stroke for that cylinder with the leaky injector, the residual compression can push its way through the nozzle spray holes, past the defective nozzle valve seat, and into the injector, injection line, and injection pump. The column of fuel in the pump/line/injector is pushed back and replaced with air. Depending on the severity of this condition, the result could be that the engine starts and runs rough for a few moments while the air purges out of the injection line, as other cylinders are not affected. In more severe circumstances, the injection line and injection pump can be filled with air. Fuel delivery to all cylinders will be affected, causing moderate to hard starting or no starting at all. This situation is a brainteaser because if only one injector is defective, the hard starting will not occur unless the piston for that cylinder with the leaky injector is on the compression stroke when the engine is stopped. For a six- or eight-cylinder engine with one bad injector, you can experience an occasional hard starting or no starting problem. The situation becomes even more puzzling if you know that no air is going into the injection pump. When trying to bleed the system, you crack the injection line nuts at the injectors and see air bubbles or foam. Troubleshooting this problem is relatively easy. Crack loose all injection line nuts at the injectors and turn the engine manually with the appropriate tools. Turn the engine so that each piston for each cylinder stops at the top of its compression stroke one at a time. For each cylinder, wait a minute and check the loosened injection line nuts for fuel movement or air bubbles. Continue turning the engine in this manner until you've placed each piston at the top of its compression stroke and you've checked for air bubbles at the injector inlet fittings. An injector causing this problem may cause other symptoms as well, such as a 'partial miss', rough running, and/or some colored exhaust. However, I have seen this problem occur with no runability or exhaust symptoms. A diesel fuel injection shop can easily test an injector's nozzle valve 'seat integrity' or 'seat tightness.'

Hard starting or no starting, moderate to heavy white exhaust

Moderate to heavy white exhaust indicates that oxygen is present and fuel is being injected. However, sufficient heat is lacking to create expansion and combustion. A worn and/or very cold engine or injection pump malfunction may cause this problem as well. In a prechamber engine with glow plugs, a failure of the glow plugs or glow plug system can cause hard starting with excessive white exhaust.

Remember that you can run into combination problems as well. A prechamber engine may be moderately worn, have a couple of burned out glow plugs, and be in cold weather. None of these conditions by themselves would necessarily cause a hard-starting problem, but each condition contributes to the problem.

Watching the exhaust while trying to start the engine or having someone look at the tailpipe for you provides valuable information as to why the problem is occurring. Some injection systems are equipped to change the timing of injection for starting or to deliver more fuel for starting. Some systems do this automatically. Other systems have an external actuator that must be moved or pressed by the operator before starting the engine. Failure to activate these devices can cause or contribute to a hard start with white smoke problem. Refer to operator manuals for instructions for your particular engine.

A pump-to-engine timing problem can cause a hard starting or no starting problem with moderate to heavy white exhaust. This problem usually occurs after an injection pump has been removed and replaced and the pump-to-engine timing was not set correctly. As described in Chapter 4, 'Moderate to heavy white exhaust with loss of power,' a prechamber engine with the pump-to-engine timing set incorrectly can be hard to start but can still run with heavy white exhaust and low power. A direct injection engine with a severe timing problem will usually not run at all but will expel white exhaust while trying to start.

A worn injection pump and/or a worn engine can also cause this problem. After an engine has been in service for a long period of time, the engine as well as the fuel injection components may show signs of wear during startup. Fuel systems are designed and calibrated to deliver an amount of fuel needed for easy starting. After the pumping unit(s) have become worn, the injection system may not be able to supply the required fuel for starting but may function normally in all other operating modes. A moderately worn engine that creates lower compression can cause or contribute to a hard starting problem with moderate to heavy white exhaust. Usually with a fuel injection system and engine worn to this point, the engine runs fine after starting and warming up. Starting becomes progressively more difficult as the unit is used and the engine and fuel injection system continue to wear.

I cannot recommend using starting fluids because of mechanical and safety concerns. Starting fluid, usually ether, when sprayed into the air intake during cranking, allows the engine to draw into the cylinder a mixture of air and atomized ether. When the piston makes the compression stroke, the air/ether mixture, and any fuel that is injected, ignites from the heat of compression to create expansion and an explosion and hopefully enough power and momentum to start the engine. However, starting fluids should never be used in prechamber engines with glow plugs because the uncontrolled explosion created in the cylinder can damage the glow plugs whether they are energized or not. Moreover, excessive use of starting fluids can also damage engine parts. If starting fluids are used at all on engines without glow plugs, they should be used sparingly, conscientiously, and safely. Ether is flammable, explosive, and when inhaled, can cause impairment or loss of consciousness.

Ambient temperature can cause or contribute to a hard starting problem with moderate to heavy white exhaust. Since the piston must compress air to create sufficient heat for combustion, if the engine is outside in cold weather, the cylinder may be unable to create enough heat for combustion. The white exhaust while trying to start confirms that the pump is pumping and that the injectors are injecting. The white exhaust also confirms that not enough heat is available at the time of injection to create sufficient expansion and combustion for starting. Some engine designs are more prone to cold weather starting problems than others. Keeping an engine warm in cold weather will make starting much easier. If a unit cannot be sheltered, various types of block heaters or coolant heaters are available.

An uncommon white exhaust problem has to do with a starting aid. Some engines are equipped with a device that sprays an amount of diesel fuel onto a heating element in the intake manifold during startup. Perkins Engine Company calls this device a "Thermostart." This device is not part of the fuel injection system. If the Thermostart is not activated before starting, hard starting or no starting with some white exhaust can occur. After startup, the device shuts off the diesel spray into the intake manifold. If the device malfunctions or is not switched off, and continues to spray diesel fuel after the engine starts, the result will be continuous white exhaust. The engine may start well, run well, and have good power, but the exhaust will be white. This problem can be very deceiving since white exhaust is generally caused by retarded pump-to-engine timing or low compression.

Be aware of the accessories on your engine or equipment. This type of problem can become very costly if the cause of the problem isn't correctly identified and unnecessary repairs are made.

Hard starting or no starting, moderate to heavy black exhaust

Moderate to heavy black exhaust indicates that heat and fuel are present. However, oxygen is lacking. The atomized fuel droplets are 'cooked' and the result is particulates, or black exhaust. This type of problem will usually be caused by a massive air restriction. If the engine does start, it will probably continue to make heavy black exhaust until the air restriction is relieved. Another possible cause of this problem is an excessive load on the engine while starting, such as a transmission or power take-off unit not permitting the engine to turn freely.

Severely worn or defective injectors can contribute to a problem of this type. Poor atomization of fuel can hamper the starting process. Depending on the heat present in the cylinder at the time of injection, the exhaust may be black, gray, or white. Injectors in this condition are in need of service or replacement and would surely cause black exhaust while the engine is warmed up and running.

Stalling problems

When a diesel engine decelerates, the fuel injection system begins to deliver fuel as the engine RPM approaches low idle. If the momentum from deceleration carries the engine RPM below the pre-set idle speed, the governor reacts to increase fuel delivery to correct idle underrun and to bring the engine back up to the correct idle RPM (see Fig. 2-31, positions 7, 8, 9, and 10, p. 29).

Stalling problems are usually blamed on the fuel system governor, and sometimes that is the case. But most often, stalling problems are associated with other runability problems, such as air in the fuel supply or retarded injection timing. In such cases, insufficient cylinder pressure is created to slow the momentum of the decelerating engine, and the engine stalls. Conditions that can cause or contribute to an engine stalling on deceleration are: air in the fuel supply; retarded injection timing; fuel supply or return line restriction; low compression; or a cold engine. If an engine doesn't stall on deceleration, but stalls after maintaining idle speed, the cause is usually: air in the fuel supply; a fuel supply restriction; a return line restriction; or an intermittent problem with voltage supplied to the on/off solenoid. Stalling problems caused by a return line restriction can occur in engines equipped with Stanadyne or Lucas-CAV distributor injection pumps.

Diesel engines and fuel system governors are engineered so that the engine maintains low idle at a specific engine RPM. Low idle speed can be adjusted if necessary and should not be lower than 25 RPM of its designed setting. Low idle RPM that is significantly lower than specifications can also cause the engine to stall on deceleration. The engine RPM gauge (tachometer) can be used to adjust low idle speed, but a separate tachometer should be used to verify the accuracy of the engine tachometer.

If an engine starts easily and runs with normal power and clean exhaust, and the low idle RPM is within specifications, but the engine stalls on deceleration, then either the injection pump or the fuel system governor will be the cause of the problem.

Chapter 7 - Turbochargers and Aneroids

One of the great developments in the evolution of the diesel engine is turbocharging. Powered by the engine exhaust, turbocharging creates a positive charge of air pressure for the engine cylinders on the intake stroke.

Fig. 7-1.
Cut-away view of a turbocharger.

1 Intake compressor wheel
2 Exhaust turbine wheel
3 Air intake from air filter
4 Pressurized air to intake manifold
5 Exhaust gas intake
6 Exhaust gas outlet
7 Lube oil supply line
8 Lube oil return line
9 Turbine shaft
10 Turbine shaft bearing(s)

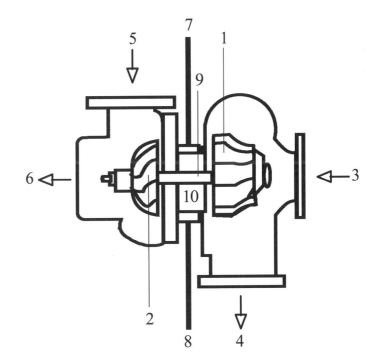

Instead of the engine pulling in air, the turbocharger builds up an amount of air pressure to feed each cylinder. The exhaust gas flow causes the turbine wheel to spin. The spinning movement is transferred to the compressor wheel by the turbine shaft. The compressor wheel creates vacuum in the air intake and also supplies pressurized air to the intake manifold. The amount of air pressure developed depends on the design of the turbocharger and the capacity of the engine. Since more air is packed into the cylinders on the intake stroke, more oxygen is available for combustion, and a greater quantity of fuel can be injected to achieve more power. The amount of load on the engine from the turbocharger is minimal. The air pressure produced by the turbocharger is called charge-air pressure, or boost.

Although a turbocharger can spin 100,000 RPM or more, the manifold pressure, or boost, does not develop instantly. An engine at idle does not develop enough exhaust gas flow to spin the turbines fast enough to create boost. Only after beginning to accelerate from idle does the turbocharger spin fast enough to create boost. This is called turbo lag, or lag time. If an injection pump is calibrated to inject a greater amount of fuel for a turbocharged engine, the full load fuel delivery can create excessive black exhaust during turbo lag. An overfueling condition would occur. A device built into the injection system can compensate for this condition and maintain the benefits of the turbocharger. The device is a manifold pressure compensator, commonly called an aneroid.

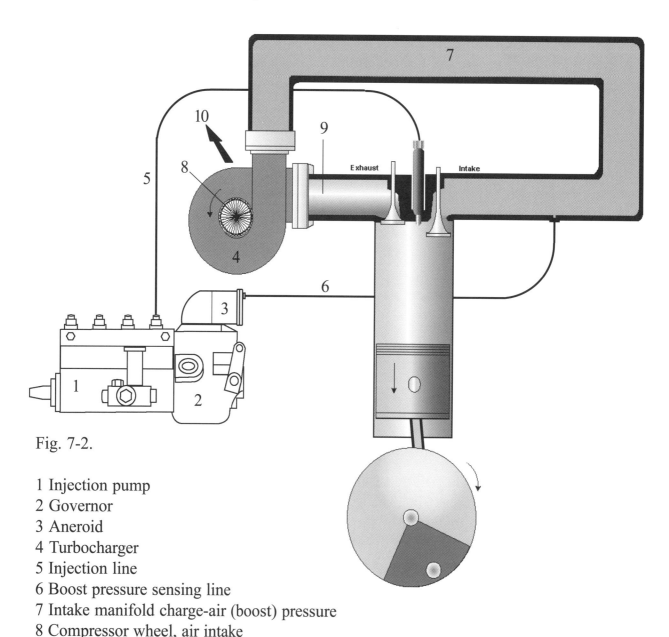

Fig. 7-2.

1 Injection pump
2 Governor
3 Aneroid
4 Turbocharger
5 Injection line
6 Boost pressure sensing line
7 Intake manifold charge-air (boost) pressure
8 Compressor wheel, air intake
9 Exhaust manifold
10 Exhaust (from exhaust turbine behind turbocharger)

Fig. 7-2 illustrates a typical turbocharged engine and aneroid set-up. The aneroid cuts back the maximum fuel available for injection until the engine begins to accelerate and the turbocharger creates boost. As the engine accelerates and the boost rises, the aneroid senses the charge-air pressure change and allows the injection pump to inject greater amounts of fuel. A pressure hose or line from the intake manifold is connected to the aneroid in the injection pump. A change in manifold pressure makes the aneroid react to cause the governor to increase or decrease the maximum available amount of fuel for injection. In a properly running turbocharged diesel engine, very little to no visible exhaust should occur during acceleration or at full load.

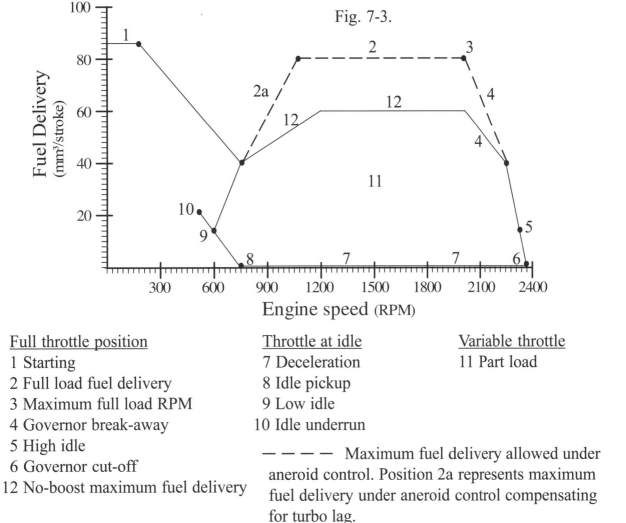

Fig. 7-3.

Full throttle position
1 Starting
2 Full load fuel delivery
3 Maximum full load RPM
4 Governor break-away
5 High idle
6 Governor cut-off
12 No-boost maximum fuel delivery

Throttle at idle
7 Deceleration
8 Idle pickup
9 Low idle
10 Idle underrun

Variable throttle
11 Part load

— — — — Maximum fuel delivery allowed under aneroid control. Position 2a represents maximum fuel delivery under aneroid control compensating for turbo lag.

Fig. 7-3 illustrates typical governor regulation of fuel delivery versus engine speed for a common fuel injection system in a turbocharged diesel tractor. The dashed lines represent the increased fuel delivery available under aneroid control. Compared to the graph in Fig. 2-31, p. 29 for a non-turbocharged engine, you can see that the turbocharged engine is able to use about 25% more fuel per injection at full load, which allows the engine to develop greater power.

Charge-air system accessories

Most turbocharger systems incorporate some form of boost limitation. Unregulated exhaust gas flow to the exhaust turbine in the turbocharger causes excessive charge-air pressure to the intake manifold during acceleration and at full load. Excessive turbo boost pressure will cause excessive compression heat and easily damage or destroy an engine. Many turbocharger systems are equipped with a device called a wastegate. The wastegate is a valve or flap that automatically opens at a preset level of boost to bypass exhaust gas away from the exhaust turbine. A wastegate can also partially restrict the flow of exhaust gases at lower engine RPMs, which decreases turbo lag. Wastegates can be part of the exhaust turbine housing or can be incorporated elsewhere in the exhaust system. Wastegates are necessary to maintain consistent charge-air pressure over the entire engine operating range.

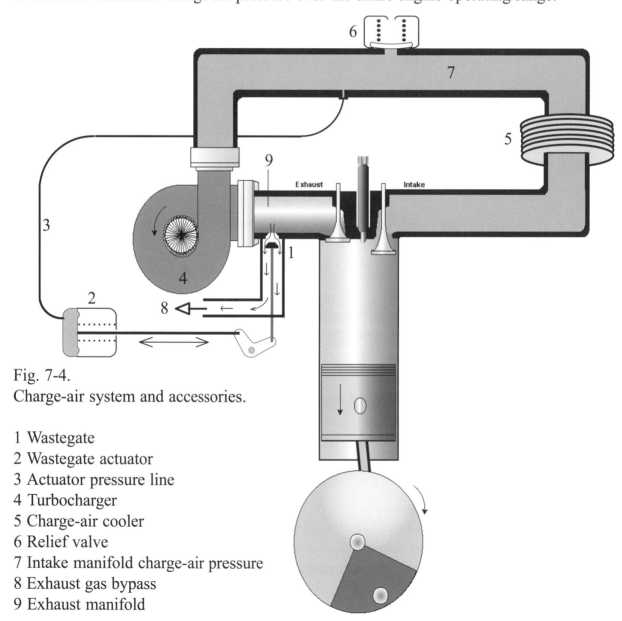

Fig. 7-4.
Charge-air system and accessories.

1 Wastegate
2 Wastegate actuator
3 Actuator pressure line
4 Turbocharger
5 Charge-air cooler
6 Relief valve
7 Intake manifold charge-air pressure
8 Exhaust gas bypass
9 Exhaust manifold

Some systems incorporate a charge-air relief valve (Fig. 7-4, position 6) as extra insurance in case of excessive turbo boost. For example, if wastegate regulation keeps the turbo boost to a maximum of 10 psi, the relief valve is set to open at 14 psi. If the wastegate fails to open, excessive charge-air pressure would open the relief valve. This event would be quite noisy and would alert the operator to the problem.

Compressing air through turbocharging creates heat and raises the charge-air temperature. The heated charge-air expands, which reduces the air (oxygen) density and hinders the effectiveness of turbocharging. Many systems are equipped with charge-air coolers (Fig. 7-4, position 5), commonly called intercoolers or aftercoolers. Charge-air coolers are heat exchangers. The cooling medium can be engine coolant, air, or water. Many marine applications use seawater to carry away heat from the charge-air. Cooling the charge-air causes the air to contract, which increases the air (oxygen) density. More oxygen in the engine cylinder means that more fuel can be injected and the engine can make more power. Charge-air coolers integrated into an engine system can increase power significantly while helping the engine to run clean. Remember from Chapter 3 that a diesel engine can have excess oxygen present in the cylinder at the time of injection. The metered and atomized fuel that is injected into the cylinder uses an amount of oxygen necessary for combustion. Any extra oxygen present has no effect on the combustion process.

The designs and variations of injection systems, turbochargers, aneroids, and charge-air systems are endless. A few common problems can develop by the failure or malfunction of a turbocharger, aneroid, or the charge-air system.

Loss of power, clean exhaust

If an air leak is present on the pressure side of the turbocharger, or in the turbocharger itself, then the boost pressure cannot develop and be sensed by the aneroid. The fuel injection system then can only deliver a reduced 'no-boost' or 'no-air' fuel quantity (see Fig. 7-3, position 12, p. 87). The exhaust will be clean, but the power will be low with this underfueling condition. If the turbocharger itself has failed and does not develop boost, then the same low-power, clean-exhaust condition will occur. Most turbocharged diesel engines have a fitting or removable plug on the pressure side of the turbocharger to attach a pressure gauge and measure boost pressure.

If the wastegate is incorrectly adjusted or is stuck open, boost pressure will not develop quickly. The aneroid will limit the maximum fuel available, causing a loss of power during acceleration from idle. At higher RPMs and working under load, sufficient boost pressure still can develop. When the aneroid senses the rise in boost pressure, more fuel will be delivered, causing a surge of power.

Although aneroids are generally very reliable components, they do fail occasionally. If the boost pressure is correct but the aneroid is slow to react, the engine will be sluggish. Complete failure of an aneroid usually keeps the maximum fuel delivery in the no-boost range, resulting in a significant loss of power with clean exhaust.

Excessive black exhaust, normal power

If the aneroid has malfunctioned to leave the fuel system able to deliver maximum fuel at all times, the result will be black exhaust on acceleration until the boost pressure rises to the point that enough oxygen is available to completely burn the fuel. Some people modify or bypass the aneroid system on an engine in an attempt to get more power while accelerating from idle. A diesel truck may produce moderate to heavy black exhaust while accelerating from a stop and then the exhaust clears up after the truck gets going. However, an ideally tuned turbocharged diesel engine should produce no more than a light haze of exhaust on acceleration and should run clean thereafter.

Some turbocharged engines have no aneroid in the fuel injection system and always expel black exhaust during acceleration from idle due to turbo lag. Failure of the turbocharger or a severe boost pressure leak in a non-aneroid system will cause an overfueling condition, some loss of power, and excessive black exhaust while working under load.

Turbochargers can be added to naturally-aspirated engines. The injection system is adjusted to deliver a greater amount of fuel at full load. An aneroid should be added if the engine expels excessive black exhaust on acceleration. Some turbocharged diesel applications don't need an aneroid because they run all day at one speed. Most other turbocharged diesel applications need an aneroid to eliminate black exhaust on acceleration during turbo lag.

The causes of turbocharger failure are numerous, but about half of the failures are caused by improper maintenance. Most turbochargers rely on engine oil for lubrication and cooling. Since a turbocharger can spin in excess of 100,000 RPM, any lack of lubrication can quickly cause damage. Dirty oil, a blockage of oil passageways, or an interruption of oil supply can cause premature failure of the turbocharger bearings and seals. A restriction of the air intake or exhaust system can make an engine run too hot and cause failure of the turbocharger and other engine parts. Keeping your engine oil, oil filter, and air filter changed regularly will help avoid premature turbocharger failure and unnecessary expense.

Turbocharged engines must run at idle for a few minutes to cool down before shutting off. If not allowed to cool down, turbocharger bearing failure or oil seal failure may result. Many turbocharged engines are equipped with an exhaust temperature sensor, or pyrometer. The pyrometer sends a signal to a gauge that allows the operator to monitor the exhaust temperature.

Failure of a charge-air cooler can also cause black exhaust. Cooling the air supplied to the engine increases the air density. More oxygen is available for combustion and the maximum fuel quantity for injection can be increased to create more power. Failure of a charge-air cooler will cause an overfueling condition and black exhaust. A small decrease in power may also be noticeable. The most common cause of charge-air cooler failure is the blockage of cooling medium passageways. This failure occurs most often in marine applications that use seawater as the cooling medium.

Blue exhaust

In Chapter 4, we saw that a bluish tint is common in the white exhaust caused by a timing or compression problem. A darker blue exhaust means that a significant amount of engine oil is burning. Failure of the turbocharger oil seals or a blockage of turbo oil passageways can cause engine oil to be pushed to the intake side of the engine manifold. Any turbocharged engine that expels darker blue exhaust should be quickly diagnosed. As with a worn-out engine that pushes oil into the combustion chamber, a turbocharged diesel engine that pushes enough oil into the engine intake can 'run away' and cause severe damage or injury. Blue exhaust can also be caused by an imbalance in the intake manifold airflow, causing oil to be pulled past the turbo oil seals. Proper air filter maintenance avoids this condition.

Superchargers

Superchargers are another type of charge-air system designed to force air into the engine cylinders. A supercharger is a mechanically driven air compressor. These units are powered by the engine, not the exhaust, and create more load than a turbocharger. However, superchargers do not create the turbo lag condition. Superchargers create boost quickly. This results in more power while accelerating from idle without excessive black exhaust.

Some newer diesel engines are equipped with a turbocharger and a supercharger. The supercharger works during acceleration from idle. After turbo boost is created, the charge-air system switches to the turbocharger. This type of system is the best of both worlds. Greater power is achieved during acceleration, as the supercharger works during turbo lag. After the turbocharger spins fast enough and the system switches the charge-air supply from supercharger to turbocharger, the extra load from the supercharger is eliminated. An aneroid becomes less necessary with this innovative design.

Rated and derated diesel engines

A rated diesel engine has the fuel injection system calibrated to deliver the maximum amount of fuel at full load that the engine can handle. Increasing the maximum fuel delivery in a rated engine creates an overfueling condition and black exhaust, as insufficient oxygen is available for complete combustion. Many engine and equipment manufacturers use derated engines in equipment that doesn't need the rated, full power capability of the engine. A derated engine has a fuel injection system calibrated to deliver less than the maximum amount of fuel that the engine can handle. A rated engine that produces 220 horsepower (HP) can be derated to produce 200 HP, 180 HP, 160 HP, etc. Engine derating is determined by the power needed for a particular piece of equipment. Overfueling a derated engine will produce more power until the maximum fuel delivery for the rated version of the engine is surpassed, causing an overfueling situation and black exhaust.

It is not advisable to increase the maximum fuel delivery for a derated engine unless recommended by the equipment manufacturer. Increasing the horsepower rating could damage the equipment and could possibly cause an unsafe situation.

Derated engines removed from equipment and installed in other equipment can have the maximum fuel delivery adjusted for the power needs of the new application.

When troubleshooting a black exhaust problem, it is helpful to know if your engine is rated or derated, since an overfueling situation will generally not cause a derated engine to produce black exhaust.

Chapter 8 - Other Types of Diesel Fuel Injection Systems

Most diesel engine manufacturers purchase fuel injection systems from companies that specialize in engineering and manufacturing diesel fuel injection systems. Robert Bosch, Stanadyne, Lucas-Varity, Zexel (Diesel Kiki), Nippondenso, and Ambac are the primary diesel fuel system manufacturers. A few engine companies have designed and developed their own fuel injection systems.

Detroit Diesel two-stroke engine and fuel system

For several decades, Detroit Diesel has designed and manufactured two-stroke diesel engines and its own unique type of fuel injection system.

The supply pump for Detroit Diesel injectors is similar to the supply pumps used in injection pump/injector fuel systems, except that the Detroit supply pumps operate at approximately 40-60 psi. Fuel supply pumps for other fuel injection systems usually operate within 5-30 psi. Diesel fuel under supply pump pressure is fed to the Detroit injectors through a common rail.

Just like other fuel systems, Detroit injectors must be fed a continuous supply of properly filtered, good quality fuel that is free of water. The fuel supply system must be unrestricted and free of air. Return fuel lines coming off the injectors and/or the supply pump are for lubrication and cooling purposes and must not be restricted.

For many years, Detroit Diesel engines were two-stroke engines. Recent production models include many four-stroke engine models. The fuel injection systems for two-stroke and four-stroke Detroit Diesel engines must still accomplish the same tasks. They must pressurize, time, and meter the fuel while the nozzle atomizes and distributes the fuel.

Let's look at the two-stroke engine and the Detroit unit injector and examine their peculiarities. Several companies manufacture two-stroke diesel engines, but Detroit Diesel has been the most common. Many variations of the two-stroke engine have been designed and manufactured in an attempt to improve on the gas exchange between strokes. We'll use a basic design of a turbocharged two-stroke engine as a model.

Starting near bottom-dead-center (BDC), the blower and turbocharger force filtered air into the combustion chamber. A blower is a mechanical air compressor driven by the engine and is similar to a supercharger.

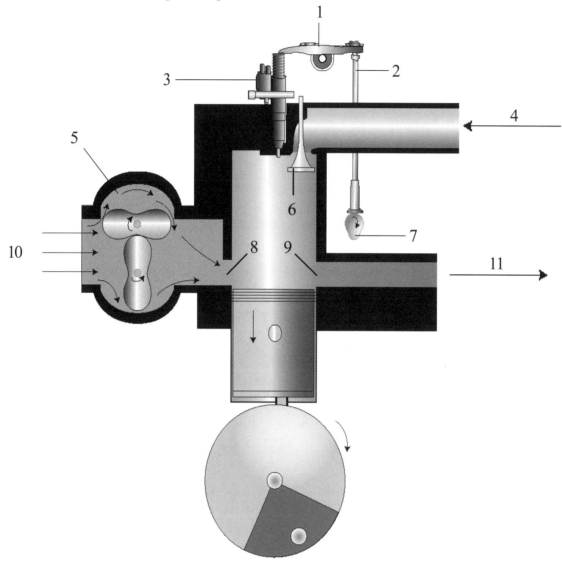

Fig. 8-1.
Detroit Diesel two-stroke engine during air induction cycle.

1 Rocker arm	4 Charge-air from turbocharger	7 Injector camshaft lobe	10 Filtered air
2 Push rod	5 Blower	8 Intake port	11 Exhaust
3 Detroit injector	6 Intake valve	9 Exhaust port	

With the piston near BDC, the intake valve is open, supplying the cylinder with charge-air from the turbocharger. The intake and exhaust ports are also open and the blower forces filtered air into the combustion chamber while forcing out exhaust gases from the previous combustion cycle.

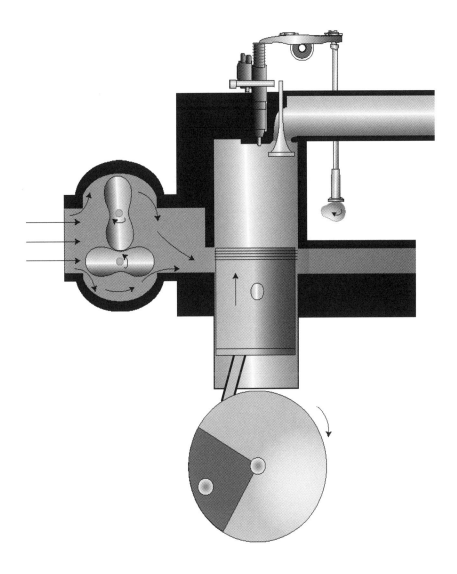

Fig. 8-2.
Detroit Diesel two-stroke engine during intake port and exhaust port closing.

     The piston moves up and closes the intake and exhaust ports. The intake valve is still open to supply charge-air to the cylinder.

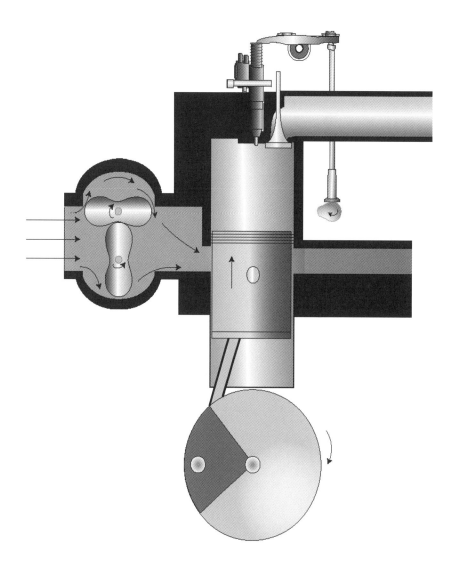

Fig. 8-3.
Detroit Diesel two-stroke engine beginning compression cycle.

The intake valve closes after the cylinder is supplied with charge-air from the turbocharger and the compression cycle begins.

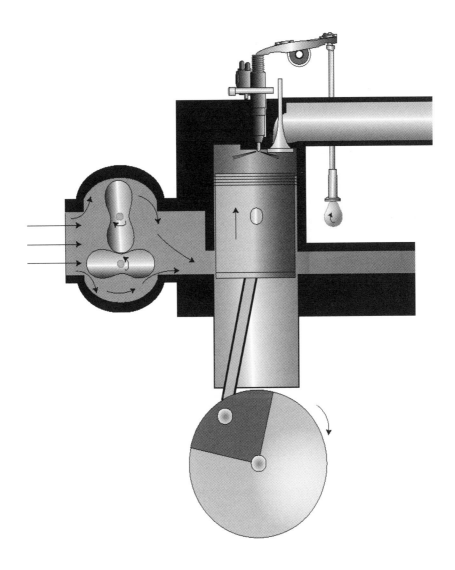

Fig. 8-4.
Detroit Diesel two-stroke engine at injection during compression cycle.

The piston moves up to compress the air in the cylinder. Near the top of the compression cycle, the injector camshaft moves the pushrod and rocker arm to compress the injector plunger and create injection pressure. A pressurized, timed, metered, and atomized burst of fuel is injected into the cylinder. Expansion and combustion begin. Like a four-stroke engine, timing is critical to make the maximum cylinder pressure occur just after TDC.

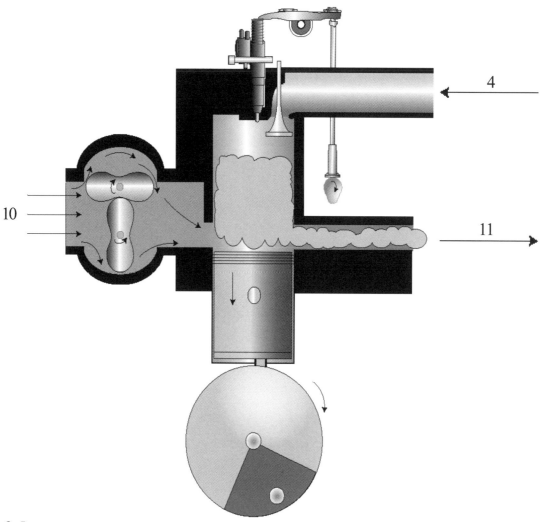

Fig. 8-5.
Detroit Diesel two-stroke engine during air induction and gas exchange cycle.

4 Charge-air from turbocharger   10 Filtered air   11 Exhaust

Expansion and combustion make the maximum cylinder pressure occur just after TDC and force the piston down for the power stroke. The intake and exhaust ports open for the gas exchange cycle, aided by the blower and turbocharger.

Many designs and methods have been used to increase the efficiency of the two-stroke engine because its biggest advantage is its power and response versus a comparably-sized four-stroke engine. With a two-stroke engine, every piston stroke creates power, whereas with a four-stroke engine, every *other* piston stroke creates power.

The greatest disadvantage of a two-stroke engine, aside from its noisy operation, is higher hydrocarbon emissions. This is due to the inherent problem of the gas exchange cycle. Blowers, air compressors, and turbochargers are used to improve the gas exchange. Air that is pressurized displaces and replaces more exhaust gases. Even so, a significant amount of exhaust gas remains in the cylinder for each compression and combustion cycle.

The Detroit unit injector has a P&B similar to an inline injection pump. Pressurization and timing of fuel delivery is done by means of a cam, pushrod, and rocker arm which compress the injector plunger, and the nozzle tip atomizes and distributes the fuel (see Fig. 8-4, p. 97). The Detroit injector is an injection pump and injector in one package. Fuel metering is accomplished by a mechanical 'rack,' which is part of each injector. Moving the rack fully to one end of its stroke will be zero delivery. Moving the rack to the other end of its stroke will be full fuel, or the maximum output for that injector model. All of the injector racks are connected to an external mechanical governor that controls starting fuel, idle, midrange, full load, high idle, and governor cutoff (see Figs. 2-31, p. 29 and 7-3, p. 87). Unless an engine is designed for a special application, a throttle device is used by the operator to control part load fuel deliveries. Fig. 8-6 is a simplified version of a Detroit injector.

Fig. 8-6. Cut-away view of a Detroit Diesel injector at port closing.

1 Plunger tappet
2 Fuel inlet
3 Fuel return (passageways not shown)
4 Plunger return spring
5 Fuel charging passageway
6 Rack
7 Plunger gear
8 Plunger and barrel (P&B)
9 Lubrication port
10 Plunger helix
11 Charge port
12 Pumping chamber
13 Spring cage
14 Nozzle (valve) assembly
15 Needle valve
16 Nozzle spray hole

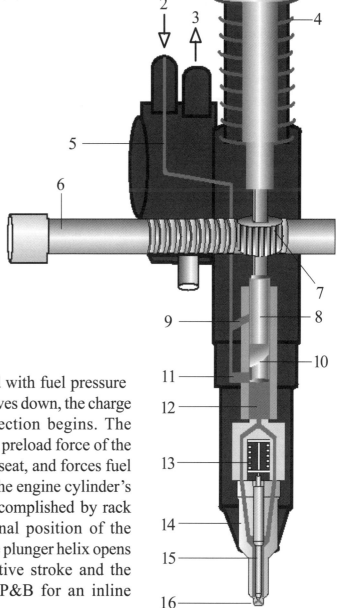

The pumping chamber is charged with fuel pressure from the supply pump. As the plunger moves down, the charge port closes and pressurization for injection begins. The injection pressure created overcomes the preload force of the spring cage, lifts the needle valve off its seat, and forces fuel through the nozzle spray holes and into the engine cylinder's hot compressed air. Fuel metering is accomplished by rack movement, which changes the rotational position of the plunger by means of the plunger gear. The plunger helix opens the charge port to determine the effective stroke and the amount of fuel delivered, just like a P&B for an inline injection pump (see Fig. 2-18, p. 19).

Detroit Diesel uses several varieties of P&Bs in its unit injectors. I simplified the illustration in Fig. 8-6 to make the functioning of the injector more understandable. No matter what design of P&B is used in a Detroit injector, the function is the same. Timing and pressurization are accomplished by the action of the cam, pushrod, and rocker arm compressing the injector plunger. Fuel metering is controlled by the movement of the rack, which determines the rotational position of the plunger and the effective stroke.

Equality of timing between all injectors is accomplished by the injector camshaft. Small adjustments are made with adjusting screws on the rocker arms to set the correct start-of-injection timing for each cylinder. Refer to your engine manual for proper tools and timing procedures.

Equality of fuel delivery between injectors is done by the manufacturer or fuel injection shop. Detroit Diesel injectors are sold or exchanged in matched sets so that the same rack positions for all injectors in a set give equal delivery within tolerance. Newer Detroit injectors use computer-controlled electronic servos instead of mechanical racks to control fuel metering.

As with a four-stroke diesel engine, poor atomization, overfueling, air restriction, and advanced start-of-injection timing cause black exhaust in a two-stroke engine. Retarded start-of-injection timing, low compression, and a cold engine cause white exhaust. Burning engine oil makes blue exhaust, and underfueling or a restriction in the fuel supply causes a low-power problem.

Air in the fuel supply can cause constant or intermittent rough running, unstable operation or surging, or can cause the engine to stall and be difficult to restart. Air can only enter the fuel supply between the fuel tank and the fuel supply pump as the supply pump is pulling fuel from the tank and creating vacuum.

If you suspect a problem with one engine cylinder or with one injector, Detroit injectors can be 'shorted out' one at a time by depressing and holding down the injector plunger tappet with appropriate tools while the engine is running. Be sure to consult your engine manual and obtain the correct tools before attempting this troubleshooting procedure and be aware of any safety concerns.

The Detroit Diesel two-stroke engine and fuel injection system is one of the simplest yet most reliable diesel systems. Complete engine and fuel system maintenance is necessary for proper running and long engine life. Two-stroke engines run inherently 'dirtier' than four-stroke engines. It is essential to use good quality fuel, maintain fuel filters and water separators, and change engine oil regularly.

Cummins PT fuel injection system

Cummins is another engine manufacturer that designs and manufactures its own unique type of fuel injection system. The Pressure/Time (PT) fuel system, or 'rail' system, consists of unit injectors and a *governed* fuel supply pump (not an injection pump). The piping and passageways that the fuel follows from the PT fuel pump to the injectors are called the 'rail,' hence the terms 'rail' system and 'rail' pressure. The PT injectors create high injection pressure by means of a cam, pushrod, and rocker arm, like a Detroit injector.

The Cummins injector contains a hydraulic pumping unit (P&B) and a spray nozzle called a 'cup.' Like all other fuel injection systems, the Cummins injector must pressurize, time, and meter fuel for delivery. The Cummins injector also must atomize and distribute the fuel into the engine cylinder's hot compressed air.

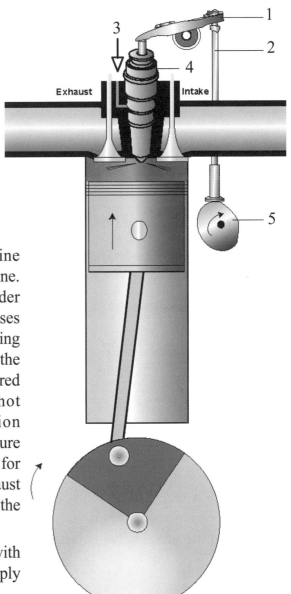

Fig. 8-7. Cummins four-stroke engine at injection during compression stroke.

1 Rocker arm
2 Push rod
3 Rail pressure from
   Cummins PT fuel pump
4 Cummins PT injector
5 Injector camshaft lobe

The Cummins four-stroke diesel engine functions like any other four-stroke diesel engine. Filtered air is drawn or forced into the cylinder during the intake stroke. The intake valve closes and the piston moves up to compress the air, creating heat. Near the top of the compression stroke, the injector delivers a pressurized, timed, and metered burst of fuel into the engine cylinder's hot compressed air. Expansion and combustion commence to make the maximum cylinder pressure occur just after TDC and force the piston down for the power stroke (see Fig. 2-17, p. 18). The exhaust valve opens and the piston moves up to push the exhaust gases out of the combustion chamber.

The Cummins PT injector is supplied with fuel by the PT fuel pump through the fuel supply rail.

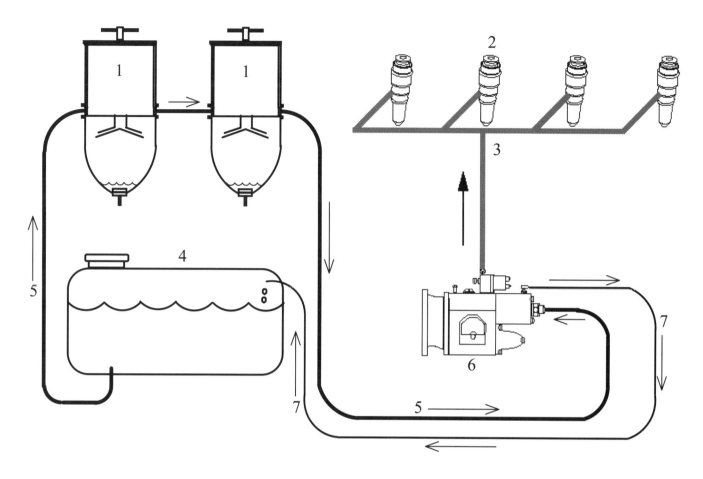

Fig. 8-8.
Cummins fuel supply and rail system.

1 Fuel filter/water separator   5 Supply line
2 Cummins PT injector   6 Cummins PT fuel pump
3 Fuel supply rail   7 Fuel return line
4 Fuel tank

    Like a supply pump, the PT fuel pump pulls fuel from the tank and through fuel filter/water separators. Since the PT fuel pump is a highly engineered piece of equipment with its own close-fitted, fast moving parts, the fuel entering the pump must be perfectly clean and free of water. The PT fuel pump moves a large volume of fuel. The amount of fuel needed for injection is relatively small and most of the fuel is returned to the tank for cooling and lubrication of the fuel pump.

    The PT fuel pump supplies fuel to the PT injectors through the fuel supply rail. Pressurization and timing of injection is accomplished by the movement of the injector cam, push rod, and rocker arm compressing the injector plunger. Fuel metering in the PT system is quite unique. To understand this concept, let's take a look at the Cummins PT injector.

Fig. 8-9.
Cut-away view of Cummins PT
injector during charging cycle.

1 Plunger return spring
2 Fuel supply pressure from
  PT fuel pump (rail pressure)
3 Lubrication slot
4 Barrel
5 Fuel charging passageway
6 Injector plunger
7 Pumping chamber
8 Injector cup (spray nozzle)
9 Spray hole

Rail pressure from the PT fuel pump enters the charging passageway and fills the pumping chamber with fuel.

The Cummins plunger and barrel is a cylindrical pump plunger fitted to a matching casing or barrel. Like all other hydraulic pumping units, the P&Bs are fitted as closely as fifty millionths of an inch, but they slide freely and very fast to pump the fuel. The lubricity of the diesel fuel is the P&B's only lubrication.

The injector cup is another version of a spray nozzle. The number and direction of spray holes in the injector cup properly distribute the fuel into the engine cylinder's hot compressed air. In a Cummins PT injector, the spray holes are usually 0.007 to 0.010 of an inch in diameter.

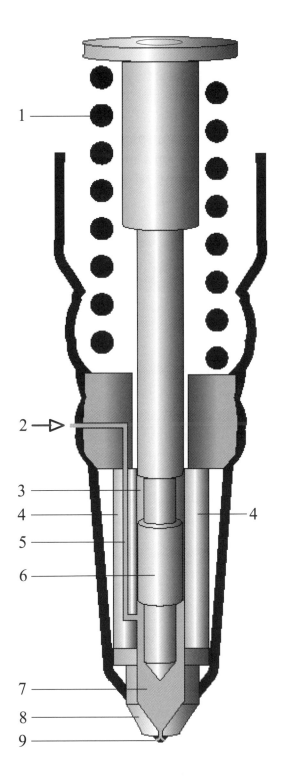

Fig. 8-10.
Cut-away view of Cummins PT injector at port closing (start of injection).

1 Plunger return spring
2 Fuel supply pressure from
  PT fuel pump (rail pressure)
3 Lubrication slot
4 Barrel
5 Fuel charging passageway
6 Injector plunger
7 Pumping chamber
8 Injector cup (spray nozzle)
9 Spray hole

The movement of the injector camshaft, pushrod, and rocker arm begins to compress the injector plunger. The plunger moves to cover the charging passageway. At this point, the pumping chamber is sealed. Any further movement of the injector plunger begins to force fuel through the injector cup spray holes and into the engine cylinder.

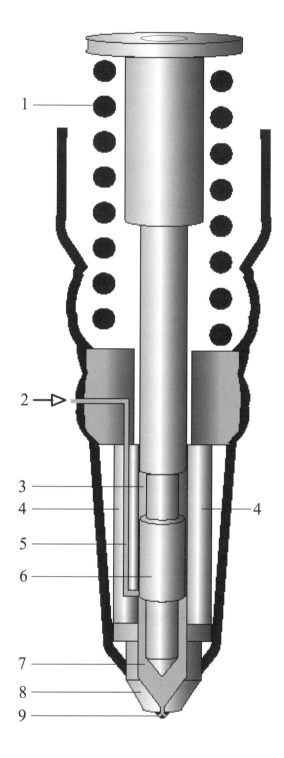

Fig. 8-11.
Cut-away view of Cummins PT injector during injection cycle.

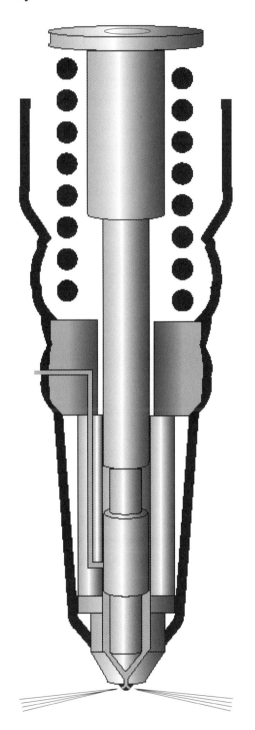

Rail pressure from the PT fuel pump enters the charging passageway and fills the pumping chamber with fuel. The movement of the injector cam, pushrod, and rocker arm quickly compresses the injector plunger. After port closing, the movement of the plunger forces fuel through the injector cup spray holes and into the engine cylinder's hot compressed air. Forcing fuel through very small spray holes creates tremendous injection pressure, 25,000 psi or more, and atomizes the fuel.

Like all diesel fuel injection systems, the Cummins PT system must pressurize, time, and meter fuel for delivery and atomize and distribute the fuel into the engine cylinder. It is apparent how this system can pressurize and time the injection of fuel by means of a cam. The PT fuel pump and PT injector work together to meter the fuel for delivery.

The PT fuel pump supplies fuel pressure to the PT injector through the rail. The rail pressure supplied to the injector is the 'pressure' part of the PT (pressure/time) system.

Consider this type of injector in an engine running at 1000 RPM. The injector makes 500 injections per minute (four-stroke engine). The injector plunger opens the pumping chamber for charging between injections. At 1000 RPM, the charging time for the pumping chamber is constant. This is the 'time' part of the PT (pressure/time) system.

If the engine RPM increases to 1200 RPM, the injector makes 600 injections per minute. The charging time between injections is shorter than at 1000 RPM. For the PT injector to deliver the same amount of fuel at 1200 RPM that it did at 1000 RPM, the PT fuel pump must increase the rail pressure so that the pumping chamber can be charged with the same amount of fuel. This relationship between rail 'pressure' and available charging 'time' is the basis for the PT (pressure/time) system.

The PT fuel pump supplying regulated rail pressure and fuel flow to the Cummins injector accomplishes fuel metering. For an engine running at 1000 RPM, increasing rail pressure increases fuel delivery and decreasing rail pressure decreases fuel delivery.

As engine RPM increases, rail pressure must increase to maintain the same fuel delivery. As engine RPM decreases, rail pressure must decrease to maintain the same fuel delivery. Fuel metering across the entire engine operating range is determined by the charging time available between injections and rail pressure.

The PT fuel pump is a governed fuel pump which changes rail pressure to affect fuel delivery. The rail pressure developed by the PT fuel pump ranges from 30 to 300 psi. The PT fuel pump governor regulates rail pressure for starting, idle, midrange, full load, high idle, and governor cutoff. Except for special applications, the PT fuel pump has a throttle device so that the operator can control rail pressure, and hence delivery, for part-load conditions. The pressure/time relationship between the PT fuel pump and PT injectors works to control fuel metering for any working moment (see Figs. 2-31, p. 29 and 7-3, p. 87).

The PT fuel pump can be tailored by the manufacturer or fuel injection shop. Rail pressure and fuel flow are calibrated to specification for a particular application. Many PT fuel pumps include an aneroid to limit rail pressure during turbo lag, which limits the maximum fuel delivery until the turbocharger creates sufficient boost.

Cummins engines in generator applications have a special governor built into the PT fuel pump to precisely regulate rail pressure and fuel delivery. Generators usually operate between 1800 to 1880 RPM. The governor must regulate rail pressure for maximum fuel delivery at 1800 RPM, for high idle at 1880 RPM, and for all part-load fuel deliveries in between. Any Cummins PT application regulates rail pressure and controls fuel delivery for any working moment. Newer PT fuel pumps include an electronic governor instead of a mechanical governor for greater precision in controlling rail pressure and fuel metering.

Equality of timing between all injectors is accomplished by the injector camshaft. Small adjustments are made with adjusting screws on the rocker arms to set the correct injector plunger depth for its corresponding piston and injector camshaft positions. Refer to your engine manual for proper tools and timing procedures. Some Cummins engines advance the start-of-injection timing for all injectors by mechanically advancing the camshaft movement to compensate for combustion lag. Fuel delivery in a Cummins PT system must commence at the right time so that the maximum cylinder pressure from expansion and combustion occurs just after TDC. Some PT systems incorporate a hydraulic device in the injector to advance the start-of-injection timing for idle to reduce white exhaust as the engine cools down.

Equality of fuel delivery between injectors is done by the manufacturer or fuel injection shop. Cummins PT injectors are sold or exchanged in matched sets so that the same rail pressure for all injectors in a set give equal delivery within tolerance.

Like all other diesel engines, poor atomization, overfueling, air restriction, and advanced injection timing cause black exhaust in a Cummins diesel engine. Retarded start-of-injection timing, low compression, and a cold engine cause white exhaust. Burning engine oil makes blue exhaust, and underfueling or a restriction in the fuel supply cause a low power problem.

The PT fuel pump pulls fuel from the tank and through fuel filter/water separators (see Fig. 8-8, p. 102). The suction side of the PT fuel pump is always creating a large vacuum while the engine is running. Any defect between the fuel tank and fuel pump, and sometimes the fuel pump itself, will pull air into the fuel supply. The Cummins PT fuel system needs a clean, unrestricted flow of fuel that is free of air.

By design, this system is prone to air ingress problems. Air bubbles in the PT fuel system can cause a non-responsive or slow-responsive throttle, constant or intermittent rough running or surging, and/or cause the engine to stall and be difficult to restart.

The engine may have some colored exhaust when air is present in the fuel supply, as the engine is struggling with itself. Depending on the amount of air in the system, each injector will deliver a different amount of fuel. Since air is highly compressible and liquid is slightly compressible, the injection pressures can vary, changing atomization and timing characteristics. The PT fuel pump is designed to bleed-off small amounts of air through the return line, but it doesn't take a lot of air in the system to cause runability problems.

If air is pulled into the fuel supply, air bubbles can collect in a filter head or at a high point in a supply line. When a filter can no longer hold that volume of air, an amount of air can pass through to the fuel pump and injectors, causing the engine to suddenly run rough, or stumble. As the engine continues running and air purges out of the system, the engine may run normally until the next shot of air passes through.

A good rule of thumb is that runability problems that come and go, or increase or decrease in severity, are usually 'air-in-fuel' problems. Air ingress problems are usually erratic, while mechanical problems are usually constant. This rule applies to all diesel fuel injection systems.

As an air leak increases, the problems become more severe. The rough running may become more constant and the engine may stumble and stall and be difficult to restart. In a severe situation, the engine will not be able to restart at all. Several methods are available to troubleshoot and pinpoint an air leak in a Cummins PT fuel system. I recommend following engine service manual procedures for troubleshooting and repairing these problems. Be sure to read all safety topics and, as always, follow safety procedures.

In conclusion, as with other types of fuel systems, the Cummins PT system needs properly filtered, good quality fuel that is free of water. The fuel supply system must be unrestricted and must not allow air to enter the fuel supply. Any return lines from the fuel pump or injectors to the tank must be clear and unrestricted. The fuel pump shut-off solenoid must be supplied with the proper voltage and the engine must be supplied with a sufficient volume of filtered air. The injectors must be correctly timed to the engine, and the engine must be in good working order and make proper compression. If a problem persists after all these requirements have been verified, only then should the PT fuel pump or injectors be considered as the cause of a problem.

Sleeve metering distributor injection pump

Robert Bosch Corporation produces a distributor injection pump that uses a sleeve metering process to control fuel delivery. The 'VE' model injection pump falls into the category of injection pump/injection line/injector. VE injection pumps are used in a wide variety of diesel applications; automotive, agricultural, industrial, and marine. Like the distributor pump described in Chapter 2, the VE pump pressurizes, times, and meters fuel delivery for each cylinder. The VE head and rotor contains a cylindrical pump plunger, or rotary plunger, fitted to a hydraulic head. As with all hydraulic pumping units, the diesel fuel is the head and rotary plunger's only lubrication.

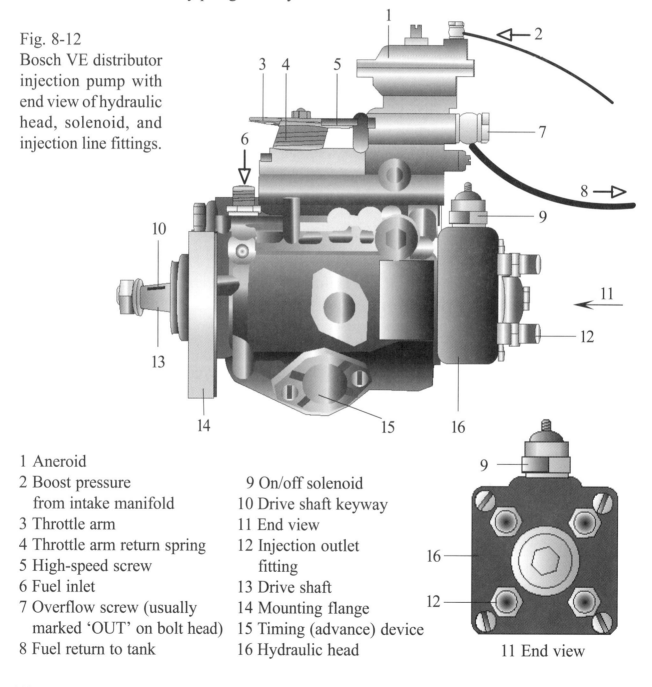

Fig. 8-12
Bosch VE distributor injection pump with end view of hydraulic head, solenoid, and injection line fittings.

1 Aneroid
2 Boost pressure
   from intake manifold
3 Throttle arm
4 Throttle arm return spring
5 High-speed screw
6 Fuel inlet
7 Overflow screw (usually
   marked 'OUT' on bolt head)
8 Fuel return to tank

9 On/off solenoid
10 Drive shaft keyway
11 End view
12 Injection outlet
   fitting
13 Drive shaft
14 Mounting flange
15 Timing (advance) device
16 Hydraulic head

11 End view

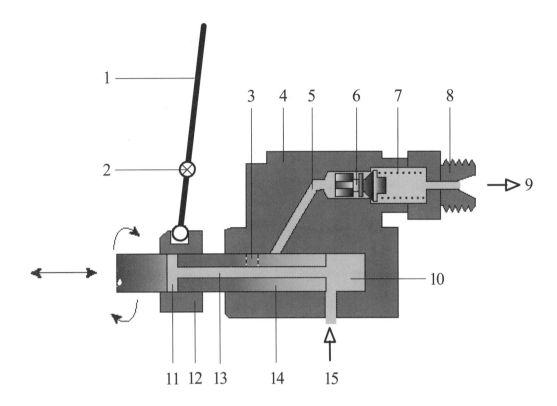

Fig. 8-13. Cut-away view of VE hydraulic head and rotary plunger with governor arm during charging cycle.

1 Governor arm	6 Delivery valve	11 Relief port
2 Governor arm pivot point	7 Delivery valve spring	12 Metering sleeve
3 Discharge port	8 Injection outlet fitting	13 Longitudinal bore
4 Hydraulic head	9 Column of fuel to injector	14 Rotary plunger (rotor)
5 Discharge passageway	10 Pumping chamber	15 Transfer pump pressure

The rotor, or rotary plunger, makes two motions, rotation and stroke. For a four-cylinder injection pump, the rotary plunger makes four strokes per one rotation, creating injection pressure for each injection outlet. The rotary plunger is connected to the injection pump drive shaft, which turns at one-half engine speed. The stroke motion of the plunger is accomplished by a cam plate, roller cage, and return springs (not shown) to push the plunger into the head to create injection pressure and to pull the plunger out between injections. The stroke motion of the rotary plunger is fixed. The rotary plunger moves the same distance into the hydraulic head for every stroke.

During the charging cycle, fuel pressure from an internal transfer pump fills the pumping chamber with fuel. The longitudinal bore of the rotary plunger and the relief port are also filled with fuel.

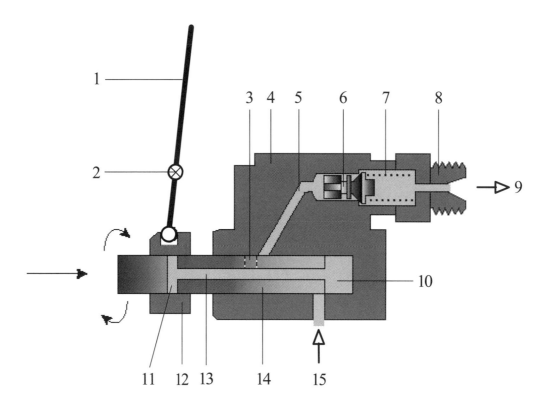

Fig. 8-14. Cut-away view of VE hydraulic head and rotary plunger with governor arm at port closing, start of pressurization.

1 Governor arm
2 Governor arm pivot point
3 Discharge port
4 Hydraulic head
5 Discharge passageway

6 Delivery valve
7 Delivery valve spring
8 Injection outlet fitting
9 Column of fuel to injector
10 Pumping chamber

11 Relief port
12 Metering sleeve
13 Longitudinal bore
14 Rotary plunger (rotor)
15 Transfer pump pressure

The rotary plunger moves into the hydraulic head and covers the transfer pump pressure inlet. At this point, the pumping chamber is sealed. Further movement of the rotary plunger creates pressure for injection. As the plunger moves into the hydraulic head, the plunger is also rotating.

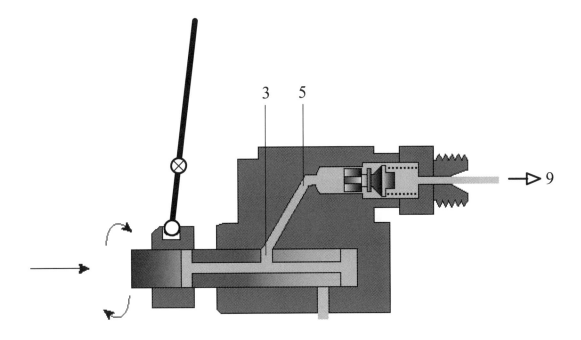

Fig. 8-15. Cut-away view of VE hydraulic head and rotary plunger with governor arm during injection.

The stroke movement of the rotary plunger pushes the plunger into the hydraulic head. The rotational movement of the rotary plunger opens the discharge port to the discharge passageway. The fuel displacement created by the stroke movement of the plunger pushes the column of fuel towards the injector and lifts the delivery valve off its seat. Injection pressure is created quickly. The pressure created by the pumping unit, transferred through the injection line, overcomes the preload force of the injector spring and lifts the needle valve off its seat. Then, after the needle valve opens, the burst of injection pressure forces fuel through very small holes in the nozzle tip. A burst of pressure forcing fuel through very small holes allows injection pressure to increase during injection (see Figs. 2-32, p. 31 and 2-33, p. 32).

Fig. 8-16.
Cut-away view of VE hydraulic head
and rotary plunger with governor arm
at port opening, end of injection.

16 Fuel spilling into pump housing
during port opening, end of injection

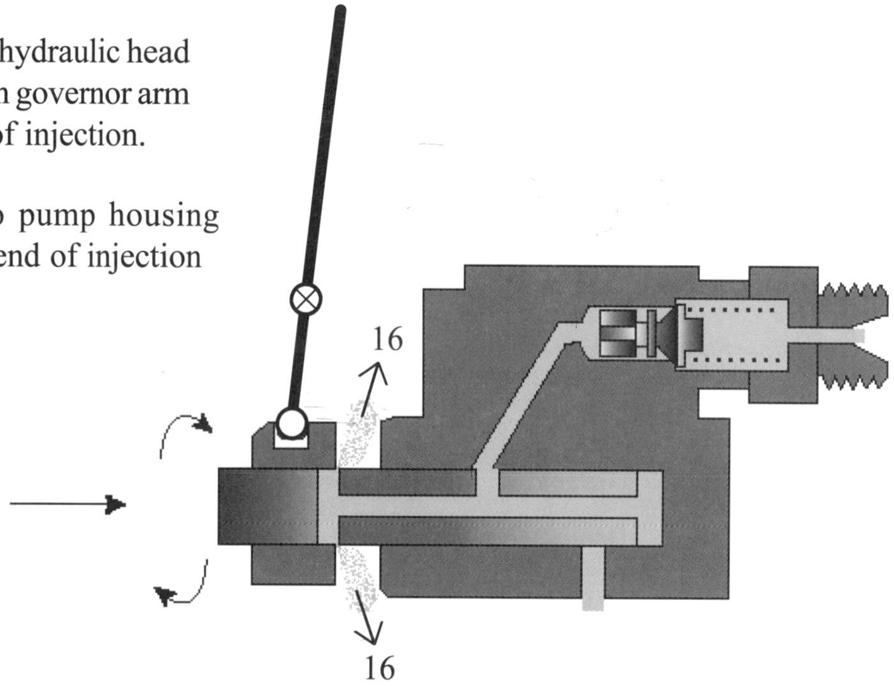

Further movement of the rotary plunger pushes the leading edge of the relief port past the end of the metering sleeve. Injection pressure is relieved into the injection pump housing and injection quickly ends.

As the engine and injection pump continue to turn, the rotary plunger moves out of the hydraulic head and the pumping chamber is charged with fuel for the next charging and injection cycle.

For a four-cylinder engine, the rotary plunger makes four injection strokes for every complete rotation of the injection pump drive shaft. As you can imagine, the pumping parts move very fast and the injection process happens very quickly. Each injection pump outlet must deliver fuel to its corresponding engine cylinder at the correct time. Depending on the engine, delivery occurs for each cylinder between 10° BTDC and 40° BTDC on the compression stroke (see Fig. 2-17, p. 18). Timing procedures for VE injection pumps vary from one engine manufacturer to the other. Consult your service manual for proper pump-to-engine timing procedures.

A characteristic of all VE injection pumps is that the injection pump drive shaft keyway points to the injection outlet that will be on the injection cycle. Looking at the drive end of a four-cylinder VE pump, if the keyway points at 10 o'clock, the injection outlet in the upper-left most position (still looking at the drive end) will be on the injection cycle. If the keyway points at 2 o'clock, the injection outlet in the upper-right most position (still looking at the drive end) will be on the injection cycle. This trick can help you set the basic pump-to-engine timing if you are rebuilding the engine or have removed the injection pump drive gear. For example, if you are installing a VE injection pump and you have previously removed the injection pump drive gear, and if number one piston is on the compression stroke at or near TDC, the driveshaft keyway must point to the injection outlet for cylinder number one. If it does not, you will not be able to set the pump-to-engine timing. Precise pump-to-engine timing is critical for the engine to run correctly. After setting the basic pump and drive gear timing, you still need to follow service manual timing procedures.

Another characteristic of all VE injection pumps is that the pump housing must be completely full of diesel fuel for the injection pump to function correctly. After bleeding the fuel supply to the injection pump and before bleeding the injection lines, crack loose the overflow screw (see Fig. 8-12, position 7, p. 108) and bleed the injection pump housing of air.

The injection outlets are in a circular formation (see Fig. 8-12, p. 108). The head and rotary plunger create injection pressure for each outlet consecutively in a circular pattern. The routing of the injection lines determines the firing order for the injection pump (see Fig. 2-29, p. 26).

A VE injection pump can have one or more timing devices to compensate for factors that affect the combustion process. For any working moment, engine speed, operating condition, and load, the timing devices will precisely adjust the start-of-injection timing so that the maximum cylinder pressure occurs just after TDC, the injected fuel burns completely, and optimum power is achieved.

Metering in the VE injection pump is accomplished by the movement of the metering sleeve. The pump governor controls the movement of the governor arm, which transfers movement to the metering sleeve. Fig. 8-17 illustrates the top of the governor arm moving to the right, pivoting on the pivot point, and the metering sleeve moving to the left. With the metering sleeve in this position, the leading edge of the relief port pushes past the edge of the metering sleeve sooner than in the previous example. Since port opening occurs earlier in Fig. 8-17 than in Fig. 8-16, less fuel is delivered.

Fig. 8-17.
Cut-away view of VE hydraulic head and rotary plunger with governor arm during injection.

1 Governor arm
2 Governor arm pivot point
9 Column of fuel to injector
12 Metering sleeve

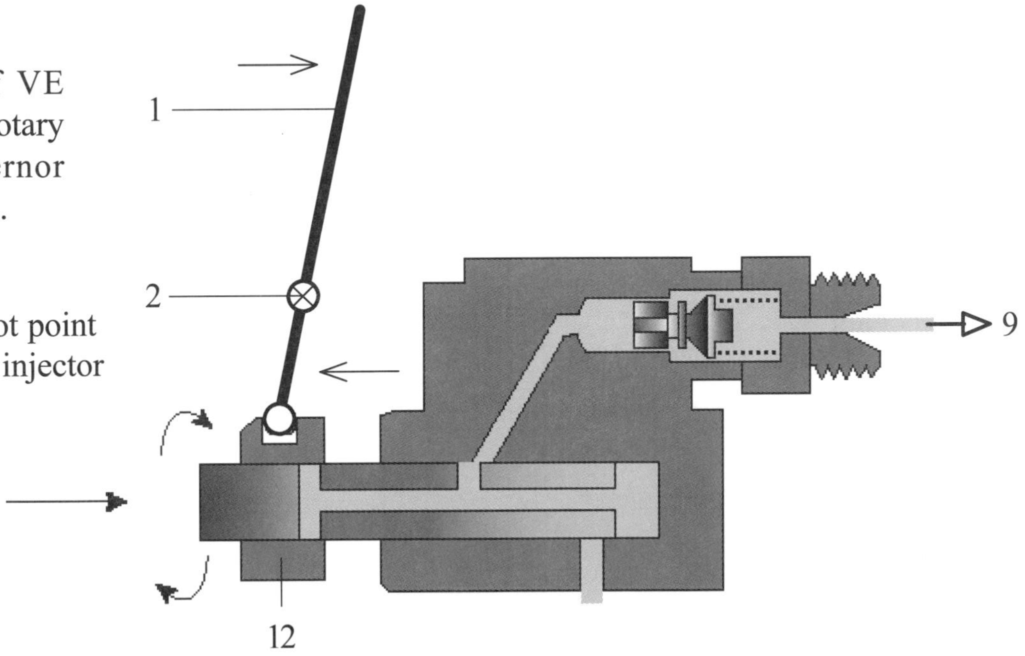

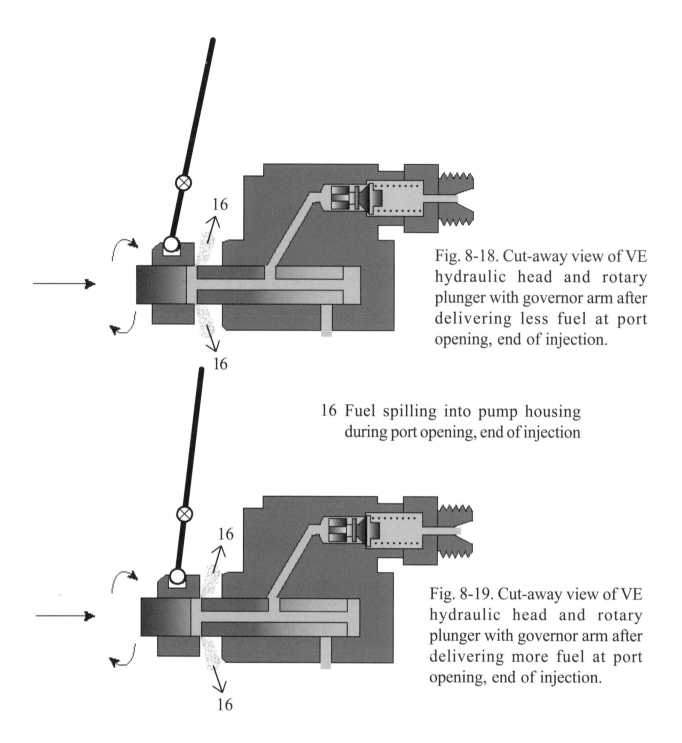

Fig. 8-18. Cut-away view of VE hydraulic head and rotary plunger with governor arm after delivering less fuel at port opening, end of injection.

16 Fuel spilling into pump housing during port opening, end of injection

Fig. 8-19. Cut-away view of VE hydraulic head and rotary plunger with governor arm after delivering more fuel at port opening, end of injection.

Figures 8-18 and 8-19 compare the two examples of a VE hydraulic head and rotary plunger at port opening or at end of injection. The metering sleeve in Fig. 8-18 allows port opening to occur sooner than the metering sleeve in Fig. 8-19. Since the metering sleeve in Fig. 8-18 allows port opening to occur sooner, less fuel is delivered than in Fig. 8-19. The injection pump governor precisely controls movement of the metering sleeve by means of the governor arm to control fuel delivery for any point in the engine operating range (see Figs. 2-31, p. 29 and 7-3, p. 87).

Delivery valves

Most injection pumps are engineered with delivery valves in the injection circuit. A delivery valve serves two basic purposes. During injection, the delivery valve is pushed off its seat and injection pressure flows around the valve. As injection pressure begins to subside, the delivery valve spring quickly returns the delivery valve back to its seat. This action helps the pressure in the injection line to drop quickly, allowing the injector needle valve to snap shut for a quick end of injection.

The other function of the delivery valve is to reduce the afterwaves remaining in the injection line. Afterwaves bounce back and forth between the injection pump and injector after injection (see Fig. 2-32, position 7, p. 32). When the delivery valve spring returns the delivery valve to its seat, a small volume of fuel is pulled back from the injection line. This movement helps to reduce the residual line pressure, thus decreasing the force of the afterwave. This process is called retraction. If a delivery valve is not functioning correctly, the wrong valve is installed, or a delivery valve spring is broken, the retraction process will not occur and the afterwave pressure will not be reduced sufficiently. If the afterwave pressure that bounces back to the injector is higher than the injector opening pressure, the injector will open and deliver fuel into the engine cylinder. Secondary injection can cause white exhaust and rough running. Some injection pumps use one delivery valve for *all* injection outlets, while other pumps have one delivery valve for *each* injection outlet. Delivery valve malfunction in an injection pump with one valve for all outlets causes white exhaust and rough running for all engine cylinders. Delivery valve malfunction in an injection pump with one valve for each outlet causes some white exhaust and a 'miss' or 'partial miss' for one cylinder.

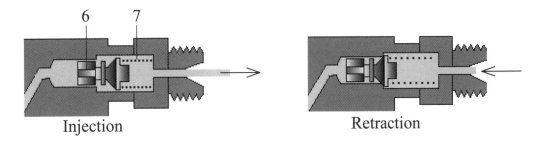

Fig. 8-20. Delivery valve movement during injection and retraction.

6 Delivery valve   7 Delivery valve spring

During the injection cycle, fuel pressure from the pumping unit pushes the delivery valve off its seat and fuel flows around the valve. After injection, the delivery valve spring returns the delivery valve to its seat and the delivery valve pulls a small amount of fuel back from the injection line for the retraction cycle. Proper movement of the delivery valve helps to create a sharp end-of-injection and a reduction in afterwave pressure.

Ambac International (formerly American Bosch and United Technologies), produces distributor injection pumps that use a sleeve metering pumping unit similar to a Robert Bosch VE injection pump. Model 100, models PSB, PSJ, and PSU injection pumps use a distributor head and rotary plunger with a metering sleeve. The biggest difference between the Robert Bosch and Ambac distributor pumping units is that the Bosch pumps contain one delivery valve for each injection outlet while the Ambac pumps contain one delivery valve for all outlets.

A peculiarity of Ambac Model 100, PSB, and PSJ injection pumps installed in four-stroke engines is that the injection pump drive turns at engine speed instead of at half-engine speed. The distributor pumping unit is geared down to half-engine speed inside the injection pump. Before removing one of these pumps for service, always set number one piston on the compression stroke and line up all timing marks according to your service manual.

Chapter 9 - Maintenance and Miscellaneous

You have seen several recurring themes regarding fuel system maintenance. Use good quality fuel that is properly filtered and free of water. Only use additives to increase the lubricity of the fuel or for cold weather, and use an algae growth inhibitor when needed. Beware of water-dispersing additives or alcohol-based additives, as they can cause more harm than good. Keep up with the required maintenance of your machine. Change fuel and air filters regularly.

Changing engine oil and oil filters

Changing oil and oil filters on time is very important for a diesel engine. Anyone who has experience with a diesel will know that the engine oil turns black within a short time after an oil change. This is due to the small amount of carbon or soot that is always created during combustion. If an oil change is delayed too long, the oil and oil filter can only hold so much of the soot. After that, the oil breaks down or starts to become abrasive and begins wearing engine parts excessively.

It has been my observation that some engine manufacturers tend to recommend a longer oil change interval than what should be required. Because so many variables are involved, only by oil analysis can you determine the optimum oil change interval for your engine. Generally, my advice to customers is to decrease the manufacturer's recommended oil change interval by 25%. If 4000 miles is recommended, change oil and filter at 3000 miles. If 200 hours is recommended, change oil and filter at 150 hours.

Let's face it. Changing oil and filter is cheap compared to an engine repair. The small investment and effort required to make more oil and filter changes will reap the benefit of a longer lasting engine. I prefer using non-synthetic oil in diesel engines, but I use high quality oil. I do not believe that the higher cost of synthetic oil justifies its benefit for a diesel, except in cold weather situations. Any oil, whether it is synthetic or natural, can only hold so much of the black soot created by combustion. After a certain point, the excessive soot in the oil becomes abrasive. My experience has shown me that using good quality oil and changing the oil and filter 25% sooner than recommended is the best formula for getting the longest life out of a diesel engine.

With the multitude of oils, oil additives, and oil treatments, keeping it simple makes the most sense. However, if you have a formula for oil, additives, and/or treatments that work for you, then keep using it. If you have been lackadaisical about oil changes, please realize that you are only costing yourself money in the long run.

In some older diesel engines, there is a necessary oil change that quite often is not done. Neglecting this oil change can result in unnecessary and costly repairs. An inline injection pump needs oil for the lubrication of certain parts (see Fig. 2-2, p. 11). The diesel fuel lubricates the pumping parts, but these types of units have internal camshafts and mechanical governors that require oil lubrication. Usually an inline injection pump is supplied with engine oil for lubrication purposes. The engine oil is constantly circulating by being fed under pressure to the injection pump and then returned to the crankcase. Although some older inline injection pumps require oil lubrication, they are not supplied with engine oil. The injection pump has its own oil reservoir or sump that requires an oil change from time to time. The engine manufacturer's service manual will include information regarding oil type, volume, and maintenance interval for an inline injection pump's oil sump.

Sometimes a person purchases an engine and no service manual is available, or manuals are lost, or not studied, etc. If you have an older diesel engine with an inline injection pump, look for an engine oil feed line that is attached to the injection pump. If no oil line can be identified, it is possible that you have an injection pump that has its own oil sump. However, some inline pumps are fed oil through passageways in the mounting flange of the pump. No oil line exists, yet the injection pump is engine oil lubricated.

It is important that you determine whether your inline injection pump is engine oil lubricated or not. Failure to regularly change the oil in an injection pump oil sump leads to premature wear and early injection pump failure.

Oil Dilution

A defect in a fuel supply system, injector, or injection pump can cause engine oil dilution, or diesel fuel entering the engine oil supply. Oil dilution becomes apparent when you notice the oil level on your engine's dipstick gradually rising. The most common cause of engine oil dilution is a leaking supply pump. Some supply pumps are mounted to the engine and driven by an internal engine camshaft. Other supply pumps are mounted to the oil lubricated part of an inline injection pump. With the drive end of the supply pump exposed to recirculating engine oil, a defective supply pump can leak diesel fuel into the engine oil and cause dilution.

Some engines are designed with the injectors and injector return lines located under the valve cover. Any external leak from an injector, injection line, or return line under the valve cover will cause engine oil dilution. Since it is usually not advisable to run an engine with the valve cover removed, this type of problem can be challenging.

Inspect all fuel connection sealing areas and replace gaskets and washers as needed. Make sure that all fuel connections are in good condition and are tightened to the correct torque. Sometimes injectors need to be removed and tested in order to find the problem. One time I had to rig up a low-pressure air connection to pressurize the injector return line system to find the problem. 5 psi of air was enough to find the leak.

Although uncommon, a P&B from an inline injection pump that is engine oil lubricated can cause dilution. The P&B is fit to very close tolerances and the lower part of the plunger is exposed to lubricating oil. If the P&B is very worn, the barrel sealing area or sealing rings in the pump housing are defective, or the barrel is cracked, fuel can leak past the plunger, past the barrel sealing area, or through the cracked barrel and into the lubricating oil. Since most inline pumps are engine oil lubricated, diesel fuel moves into the engine oil crankcase and the oil level begins to rise. A P&B in this condition will certainly cause a noticeable 'miss' or a 'dead miss.' A plugged injector or injection line can cause the barrel of a P&B to crack. It is vital to check the injector and injection line for that cylinder with the cracked P&B or the same thing will happen after the injection pump is serviced. It is always prudent to test all injectors while an injection pump is serviced or replaced.

Diesel engines equipped with distributor injection pumps can experience oil dilution caused by excessive wear of the pump drive shaft, drive shaft bearing, or drive shaft seal. Most distributor pumps are gear driven with the drive end of the pump exposed to recirculating engine oil. Because distributor pumps are lubricated internally only by diesel fuel, failure of the pump drive or drive shaft seal can allow fuel to leak into the crankcase. Unless an engine is equipped with an engine-driven supply pump, the distributor pump drive or drive shaft seal will be the cause of dilution.

Before removing any injection pump from an engine for repair or replacement, it is advisable to set number one piston on the *compression stroke* at or near TDC and line up all timing marks. Timing procedures vary. Some systems set number one piston at TDC, while other systems set number one piston before TDC. Consult your engine service manual for proper timing procedures. Setting the engine and injection pump on the timing marks before removing the injection pump makes re-installation much easier.

Stanadyne model 'DB' distributor injection pump drive shaft and seals

Usually the injection pump drive shaft remains in the pump when the injection pump is removed. When removing some older Stanadyne model 'DB' distributor injection pumps from the engine, the pump drive shaft remains on the engine. Be sure to set number one piston on the compression stroke and line up the timing marks in the injection pump timing window. As a precaution, wire the injection pump throttle arm held in the full throttle position so that the governor weights in the injection pump won't slip out of place. After the injection pump is removed, make sure that the engine does not turn, as the injection pump drive gear will not be supported and damage could result. After the 'DB' injection pump has been tested, serviced, or replaced, several precautions are necessary for correct installation.

Before installation, the timing marks should be lined up in the pump timing window and the throttle arm should be wired and held in the full throttle position. The engine will be set correctly with number one piston on the compression stroke at or near TDC because you did that before removing the injection pump.

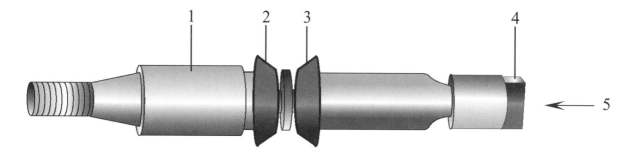

Fig. 9-1. Stanadyne model DB drive shaft and drive shaft seals.

1 Bearing support area
2 Drive shaft oil seal
3 Drive shaft fuel seal

4 Drive shaft tang
5 End view of drive shaft tang (Fig. 9-2)

Fig. 9-1 illustrates a typical drive shaft and drive shaft seals for a Stanadyne model DB distributor injection pump. After removing the injection pump from the engine, the drive shaft remains attached to the injection pump drive gear.

Before re-installing the injection pump, thoroughly clean the pump flange mounting area and remove any old mounting seals or gaskets. New mounting seals or gaskets should be supplied with your injection pump after testing, service, or replacement.

The old drive shaft seals must be removed and replaced with new seals. Drive shaft seals are made of a flexible rubber-type material. An installation sleeve is available from your fuel injection shop to easily slide the new seals over the drive shaft and into place without damaging the seals. Make sure the new seals are installed as shown, facing back-to-back. The left seal in Fig. 9-1 keeps engine oil out of the injection pump. The right seal keeps diesel fuel in the injection pump. Each seal must be installed in the correct notch on the drive shaft. Use light grease or STP engine oil treatment as lubrication when installing the new drive shaft seals. I prefer using STP because it is very slippery and makes seal installation and pump installation much easier.

After the new drive shaft seals are installed, look at the end of the drive shaft tang. The locating dot on the end of the drive shaft tang must correspond to the locating dot in the injection pump drive shaft tang slot (see Fig. 9-2, p. 121). If the timing marks are lined up in the injection pump timing window and the number one piston is on the *compression* stroke at or near TDC, the locating dots will correspond. Only if the injection pump drive gear has been removed and not re-installed correctly will the locating dots not correspond. In such a case, refer to your engine service manual for correct gear timing procedures.

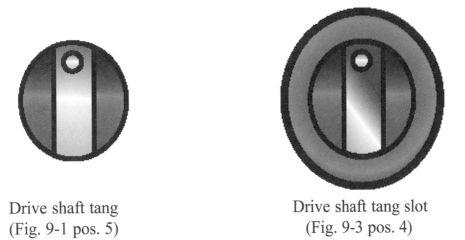

Drive shaft tang
(Fig. 9-1 pos. 5)

Drive shaft tang slot
(Fig. 9-3 pos. 4)

Fig. 9-2. End view of drive shaft tang and view of drive shaft tang slot looking inside the injection pump pilot tube. Locating dots must correspond before pump installation.

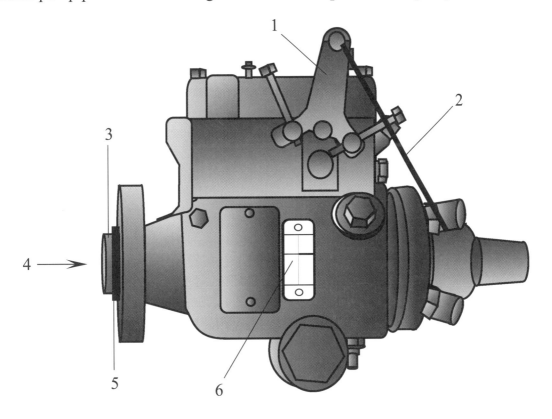

Fig. 9-3. Stanadyne model 'DB' distributor injection pump.

1 Throttle arm
2 Wire holding throttle arm in full throttle position
3 Pilot tube
4 View of drive shaft tang slot in Fig. 9-2
5 Mounting seal
6 Timing window with timing marks aligned

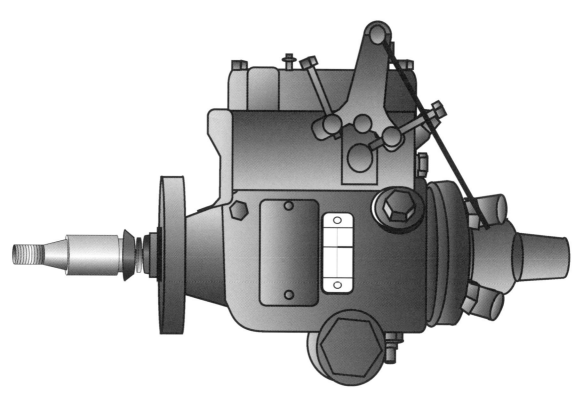

Fig. 9-4. Installation of Stanadyne model 'DB' injection pump onto drive shaft.

With new drive shaft seals installed, number one piston on the compression stroke at or near TDC, the timing marks aligned in the injection pump timing window, and the locating dots corresponding on the end of the drive shaft tang and in the drive shaft tang slot, you are ready to install the injection pump onto the pump drive shaft.

Liberally coat the drive shaft seals and pilot tube with light grease or STP. The pilot tube is made of brass. As you move the injection pump onto the drive shaft, be very careful not to damage the brass pilot tube. When the pilot tube reaches the leading edge of the drive shaft fuel seal, the seal must be compressed or carefully tucked into the pilot tube. A tool is available from your fuel injection shop to compress the drive shaft fuel seal as you move the injection pump onto the drive shaft. If no tool is available, you can use your fingers or a pencil eraser to carefully tuck the leading edge of the drive shaft fuel seal into the pilot tube. Slowly move the injection pump over the fuel seal. Carefully pull the injection pump back slightly to the position shown in Fig. 9-4. Have a mirror and light ready to check the fuel seal on the back side of the drive shaft. It is very easy to fold over the drive shaft fuel seal and if the seal is going to fold over, it will happen where you can't see it. You may need an extra hand to double-check the fuel seal on the back side of the drive shaft with a light and a mirror, but the extra effort is well worth it. If the injection pump is installed with the drive shaft fuel seal folded over, engine oil dilution will occur quickly after the engine is running. The pilot tube will also be damaged. The injection pump must then be removed again and taken back to the fuel injection shop for further repairs. Having the patience to correctly install this type of injection pump will save you money, time, and grief.

After you've confirmed with a light and a mirror that the drive shaft fuel seal has been tucked completely into the pilot tube, continue to slowly and carefully move the injection pump onto the drive shaft. The drive shaft oil seal is facing opposite the fuel seal and will compress itself as the pilot tube moves over it. The bearing support area of the drive shaft (see Fig. 9-1, position 1, p. 120) will be closely fit to the inside diameter of the pilot tube. The pilot tube and bearing support area of the drive shaft are actually the support bearing for the drive shaft and drive shaft gear. After the pilot tube has moved over the bearing support area of the drive shaft, you will feel the drive shaft tang engage into the drive shaft tang slot. A slight twisting movement of the injection pump may be necessary to get the drive shaft tang into the tang slot. If the injection pump mounting flange comes flush with the pump mounting area on the engine, you will know that the drive shaft tang has engaged the tang slot. Never force the injection pump to come flush with the mounting area. If the drive shaft tang did not engage the tang slot, you must carefully remove the injection pump and start over. Following these steps should help to make a successful installation on the first try. Consult your engine service manual to review all installation procedures and precautions.

After the injection pump comes flush with the pump mounting area on the engine, use appropriate fasteners to secure the injection pump to the engine. If the timing marks in the injection pump timing window are not aligned at this point, adjusting slots in the pump mounting flange allows you to turn the injection pump to line up the timing marks.

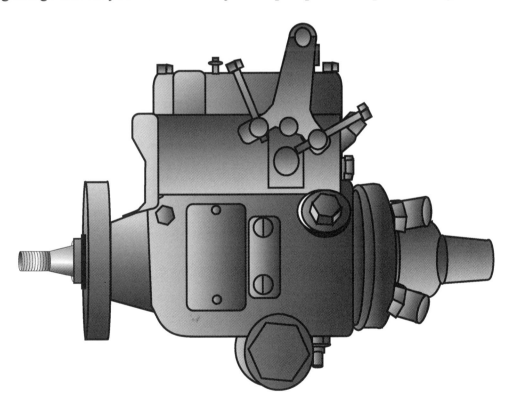

Fig. 9-5. Installation completed of Stanadyne model 'DB' injection pump onto drive shaft.

Once the injection pump is secured to the engine, replace the timing window and gasket. Do not over-tighten the timing window screws. Tighten the timing window screws slightly until the timing window gasket begins to squash. Over-tightening of the timing window screws will strip the aluminum threads in the injection pump housing. Remove the wire holding the throttle arm. Review your engine service manual procedures for completing the installation and for bleeding the fuel supply before starting. Look at the exhaust after the engine is warmed-up and running. A small timing adjustment may be needed.

After the engine is warmed-up and running, if you see a small amount of white exhaust while the engine is working and under load, you will need to slightly advance the pump-to-engine timing. To advance the pump-to-engine timing, the pump housing must be turned opposite the rotation of the drive shaft. If the pump drive shaft turns clockwise (looking at the drive end of the injection pump), the pump housing must be turned counter-clockwise (looking at the drive end of the injection pump) to advance the pump-to-engine timing. Make marks on the injection pump mounting flange and pump mounting area on the engine before making this adjustment. You may need to return the static timing to its original position, which you set by lining up the timing marks in the timing window with number one piston on the compression stroke at or near TDC. If advancing the pump-to-engine timing a few degrees gets rid of the white exhaust, then the injection pump is correctly timed to the engine. Remember that the injection pump must be secured to the engine while starting or running. Never try adjusting the pump-to-engine timing while the engine is trying to start or is running.

With all injection pump installations, in addition to following service manual procedures, I recommend replacing all fuel filters, and verifying that the injection pump has a positive flow of fuel at the pump inlet without air in the fuel supply, and that any return lines are clear and not restricted. For Stanadyne and Lucas-CAV distributor injection pumps, a restricted return line from the injection pump can cause a loss of power and rough running, usually with white exhaust.

It is also advisable to have the injectors tested while the injection pump is being serviced. Make sure that all injection lines are blown out with compressed air and that no foreign material enters the injection lines, injection outlet fittings, or injector inlet fittings during installation.

Fuel leaks

Diesel fuel injection and fuel supply systems can leak for a variety of reasons. It is important to find the source of the leak before making repairs because diesel fuel can travel almost invisibly on a surface. A small fuel leak in an area not readily visible can travel down and start dripping off of a lower point. Although you may think you have spotted the source of the leak, it is quite possible that the leak is occurring at a higher point. If a unit is especially dirty or greasy, cleaning will make the job much easier. Never clean or spray water or liquid on an engine while it is running. Water sprayed on an engine or injection pump can cause a sudden change in the temperature of the metals and seize a pumping unit or cause other engine damage.

When looking for the source of a leak, it is helpful to use compressed air. Spray compressed air on an area wet with fuel (wearing safety glasses or a face shield, of course). Using a light, look for the fuel to return. When the surface gets wet with fuel again, spray compressed air to dry it off, but look for other wet areas higher than your initial point. Continue using compressed air and drying off areas until you've reached the source of the leak. A very small leak and easy repair can initially look like a huge problem. Take the time to identify the source of the leak. This procedure is done with the engine running, so be aware of all safety concerns.

Parts, gaskets, and/or seals usually need to be replaced to correct a leak. If your injection pump is leaking, talk with your fuel injection shop first. Occasionally a small repair can be made on an injection pump without removing it from the engine. The correct parts, whether they be seals, gaskets, washers, etc., must be obtained, and many fasteners on an injection pump require a specific tightening torque. Write down all of the numbers on the injection pump tag before talking with a fuel injection shop.

If you've determined that a defective injection line is causing the problem, be sure to replace it with exactly the same part. Even though you may get another injection line to fit, any change in the inside diameter or the length of the injection line from the original may cause a rough running problem, premature wear, and ultimately failure of your injection system.

If an injector is determined to be the cause of a leak, the injector should be removed and taken to a fuel injection shop for repair or replacement. If an injector is to be replaced, make sure to replace it with exactly the same part. When replacing injectors for any reason, make sure that all compression sealing areas in the engine are clean. Many injectors use a copper or other soft metal compression washer to seal the cylinder from compression leaks. Always use a new compression washer when installing injectors. Any other o-rings, washers, and gaskets on an injector should be replaced before installation. Follow service manual procedures for any other installation concerns and torque values.

When replacing any engine part or fuel injection part, make sure that you use parts that are original equipment (OE). I cannot recommend using aftermarket parts, except glow plugs, because in my experience, some aftermarket parts are good and some are not. Only if I have good, previous experience with a particular aftermarket part, will I recommend using it.

Pumping unit seizure

The pumping units of any diesel fuel injection system are close-fitted, fast moving parts that produce high-speed, high-pressure, hydraulic pumping. The only lubrication for these pumping units is the diesel fuel itself. For a variety of reasons, a pumping unit can bind up or seize. Pump seizures are unfortunate and costly, but are usually avoidable.

The main cause of a pumping unit seizure is lack of lubrication. Diesel fuel contaminated with water or fuel that is low in viscosity will not provide the necessary lubrication. It doesn't take long for a pumping unit to seize once the lubrication from the fuel is lost. It is critically important to supply your fuel system with perfectly clean, water-free fuel of appropriate viscosity.

Pumping units can seize because of improper installation and/or misalignment. If a distributor injection pump is incorrectly installed or the mounting fasteners have loosened while running, a side thrust can be transferred to the pumping unit. With the injection pump turning at several hundred RPM, a small misalignment can transfer enough force on the pumping unit to overcome the tiny layer of lubrication in the pumping unit and make the hydraulic metal parts rub against each other. Seizures happen very fast and a small mistake can cost several hundred dollars. When installing an injection pump or injectors, follow all service manual installation procedures exactly. Make sure that all mounting surfaces are free of dirt, grease, and old seals or gaskets. Replace all old mounting gaskets and/or seals. Torque any mounting fastener for pumps or injectors to the recommended value in your engine manual. Never change the injection pump timing while the engine is running. All injection pump and injector fasteners or holddowns must be secure when the engine is running or trying to start.

In pump/line/injector systems, pumping units can seize because of a restriction in the injector, or because an injector does not open. If contaminated fuel has been used, the hydraulic parts of an injector can stick or become frozen. The high-pressure burst from the injection pump will not open the injector and deliver fuel into the cylinder. Because the high-pressure burst has nowhere to go, it quickly rebounds and returns to the pumping unit, causing a slight distortion in the hydraulic parts, and thus the unit seizes. For an inline injection pump, a P&B can seize or the barrel can crack, causing a 'miss' and engine oil dilution. An injector with the opening pressure adjusted too high and which cannot open will cause the same predicament. Never try to change the injector opening pressure unless you have a suitable injector tester and proper instructions. While testing an injector, keep your hands clear of the high-pressure spray which can penetrate skin and cause blood poisoning. Always set the opening pressure to factory specifications. If an injection line is removed from an engine and left outside exposed to the elements, it can get plugged with dirt and/or get wet. Rust can form inside the small diameter bore of the injection line and cause it to be plugged. Using a plugged injection line will also cause a pumping unit seizure. When removing fuel system components from an engine, use plastic caps to cover all fuel connections.

Keep injection lines in plastic bags and use compressed air to blow them out before installing. When installing fuel system components, make sure that all fuel connections are clean, injection lines are clear, and fasteners are tightened to the appropriate torque.

An uncommon cause of pumping unit seizure can occur in certain distributor injection pumps. If the injection line attached to the injection pump has a banjo fitting and banjo bolt, two washers are needed on each side of the banjo fitting before tightening. A banjo fitting is so named because of its shape, which resembles a banjo. A banjo bolt is a hollow flow-through screw.

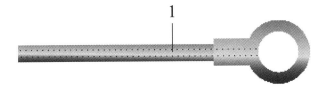

Fig. 9-6. Injection line with banjo fitting.

1 High-pressure passageway

Fig. 9-7. Cut-away view of banjo bolt

Fig. 9-8. Injection line with banjo fitting, banjo bolt, and sealing washers.

1 Banjo bolt
2 Sealing washers

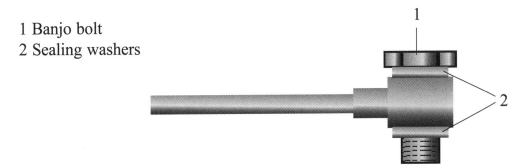

The sealing washers squash a bit when torqued to seal the high injection pressure. If a flattened or non-original washer is used, or if one of the two washers is missing and the banjo bolt is tightened, the end of the bolt can bottom in the threaded hole and put pressure on the wall of the pumping unit. Pump seizure occurs quickly when trying to start the engine. When removing injection lines with banjo fittings, always replace the banjo bolt washers with new OE washers and tighten the banjo bolt to the correct torque. If a leak is found in the area of the banjo fitting, it is preferable to stop the engine and replace the washers before retightening the banjo bolt.

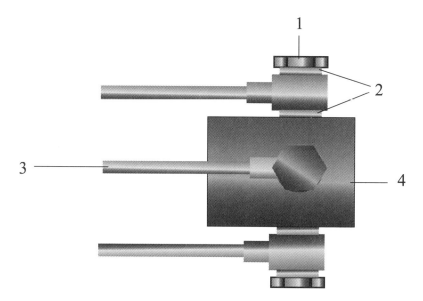

Fig. 9-9. Hydraulic head with injection lines, banjo fittings, banjo bolts, and sealing washers.

1 Banjo bolt
2 Sealing washers
3 Injection line with banjo fitting
4 Hydraulic head

Glow plug system troubleshooting

As previously discussed, glow plugs preheat the combustion chamber for a prechamber engine during start up. The glow plug uses battery current to create heat quickly before cranking. The element in the glow plug tip creates an electrical resistance so that the battery current turns into heat. Testing and/or replacing glow plugs should be part of a regular maintenance program. Generally, 20,000 to 40,000 miles or 400 to 800 hours are good inspection intervals. Glow plugs used for long periods of time without being removed and inspected can result in costly repairs. Although a glow plug usually fails before it breaks, I have seen severe engine damage caused by an old glow plug breaking off into a cylinder. Also, old glow plugs can break while being removed. A small effort now can save costly repairs later. Glow plugs that show distortion, bubbling, or other wear on the glow plug tip should be replaced.

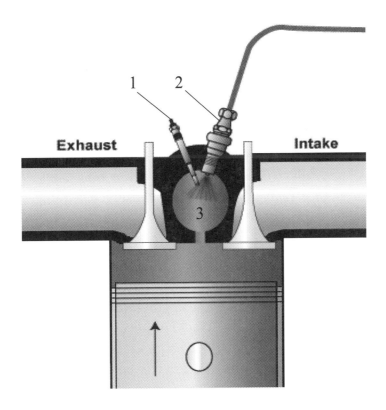

Fig. 9-10. Prechamber engine cylinder with glow plug.

1 Glow plug
2 Injector
3 Prechamber

If glow plug failure is suspected, as in a hard starting with white exhaust problem, several easy tests can be made to identify or eliminate possible causes. These tests are done while the engine is not running.

With a 12-volt test light, attach the test light clip to the battery ground or other suitable ground. Remove a wire connector from a glow plug and touch the test light probe to the wire connector or clip. Turn your ignition or engine controls to 'on' or 'preheat,' but don't start the engine. The test light will show if voltage is being delivered through the glow plug wire. Some glow plug controllers will cycle voltage at intervals to the glow plugs. Usually you can hear the switch working in the glow plug controller.

If the test light shows that the glow plugs are receiving voltage, the glow plugs can be tested to see if they are working. Remove the wire connectors or clips from the glow plugs, attach the 12-volt test light clip to the positive terminal of a 12-volt battery, and touch the test light probe to the glow plug terminal. If the test light shines brightly as if it were touched to the battery ground, then the glow plug has continuity and is probably good. A dim light or no light means that the glow plug is definitely bad.

These tests can also be done with a digital multimeter. Testing for voltage to the glow plug is easy. Set the meter to a proper direct voltage range, touch the positive probe to the glow plug wire connector and touch the negative probe to the battery ground or other ground while the ignition is set to 'on' or 'preheat.' To test for glow plug resistance or continuity, set the multimeter to 0.1 ohms or below. Touch the positive probe to the glow plug terminal and touch the negative probe to the glow plug body. A normal resistance reading for a cold glow plug is 0.1 to 1.0 ohms. After you've tested all the glow plugs, any glow plug that has a significantly lower resistance than the rest, or no resistance reading, can be replaced. Glow plug system failures are the most common cause of a hard starting with white exhaust problem in a prechamber engine.

The glow plugs themselves can be used as a troubleshooting tool in certain circumstances. If a prechamber engine equipped with glow plugs develops a consistent roughness or 'miss,' and the engine produces white or gray exhaust, then one or more cylinders may have a timing or compression problem. Cracking injection line nuts one at a time and noticing the change in the running of the engine is a good test for this condition. However, for a prechamber engine, the glow plugs themselves can be used as a probe. After starting the engine, remove the glow plug wire connectors from the glow plugs. Using a digital multimeter that can read 0.1 ohms or less, test the resistance of each glow plug as described in the previous paragraph, but while the engine is running. The cylinders that make more heat will have a higher glow plug resistance reading. The colder cylinder(s) will have a lower glow plug resistance reading. The glow plugs must be in good condition and show continuity and/or resistance to make this test possible. It's a neat trick and a fast way to find a blown head gasket, bad engine valve, worn cylinder, etc. As always, follow good safety practices and use common sense when working on or around a running engine.

Excessive engine idling

Another important topic is excessive engine idling. Many will find it hard to believe that letting your diesel engine run at low idle for extended periods of time is absolutely the worst thing you can do for your engine. Tests have shown time and again that an engine wears the most during extended idling periods. Low idle is the most unstable running condition. Less heat is generated, causing incomplete combustion and excessive deposits in the cylinder. Excessive engine idling also creates more pollution.

Many diesel engine owners have come to the false conclusion that a diesel engine is better off idling than being shut off. This probably comes from observing truckers who keep their engines idling for extended periods of time. A trucker could have many reasons for keeping an engine running. A turbocharged engine needs to cool down before being shut off. A trucker may be living in the rig and needs the engine to supply power for heat, air conditioning, or electricity. The trucker may need power from the engine for other purposes as well. However, only in severely cold weather would it be preferable to keep an engine idling rather than shutting it off. Even in a cold weather situation, it would be best to have a solenoid or some other device installed to raise the engine RPM to 900-1200 RPM instead of idling at 500-800 RPM. Similarly, when power is needed at idle to run a heater, air conditioning, etc., it is best to have the engine RPM set higher than low idle. The wear on the engine is dramatically reduced.

I received a call one day from the owner of a towing company who used two Ford trucks in his fleet which were equipped with 7.3-liter Navistar diesel engines. I had previously serviced an injection pump and injectors for one of the two trucks. The owner was a little upset when he told me that he just had the pump and injectors serviced and the engine still smoked and had low power. I asked what color the exhaust was and he said it was white. After talking with the mechanic and being satisfied that the pump was correctly timed to the engine and that the fuel supply and fuel return were in good working order, I asked to talk with the owner again. I told him that if the information I received from his mechanic was correct regarding the timing and the fuel supply and return lines, then the next step would be a compression test.

The silence of the next few moments was followed by the sound of disbelief. The owner insisted that something had to be wrong with the injection pump or injectors because the engine only had 50,000 miles on it. I had worked on his fuel system just a few days earlier and was confident that it was working correctly. I told him that I would give him another injection pump and set of injectors to try if he wanted, provided that his mechanic first performed a compression test.

Later that day, I received a call from the towing company owner, who had renewed his faith in me. He said, "Bob, you're absolutely right. All eight cylinders are low on compression. This engine is worn out. Just how the heck did this happen?" My first question was, "Do your operators let the engines idle for extended periods of time?" The owner said,

"Of course. They're diesels!" I explained to him how excessive idling could cause premature wear, but that this was the most extreme case I had ever encountered. I also pointed out that an idling engine does not put miles on the odometer. I asked if I could inspect the engine parts after they removed and tore down the engine. The owner said to drop by anytime the following day. I felt badly for the man, but I was also relieved that the problem was not caused by my work. I took a long lunch the next day and visited the towing company's shop. I greeted the mechanic and he showed me the engine parts. All the cylinder walls were worn, discolored, and glazed. Normally, a cylinder wall has a silvery surface. The piston rings were severely worn, as well. The root cause of this premature wear was the excessive engine idling. The mechanic was very experienced and he knew about the perils of excessive idling. The towing company operators had scoffed at him when he requested that they not idle the engines so much. "It's a diesel! They're made to idle all day," he was told. Nothing could be further from the truth.

Needless to say, that towing company doesn't let its trucks idle unnecessarily anymore. In addition, the owner chose to follow my advice on better filtering and water separation, so I equipped their fleet of trucks with better-than-original water separators. The mechanic liked my view on more frequent oil changes, so they decreased the oil change interval by 25%. I recommended one particular fuel source which sold the best quality fuel in the area and which was very conscientious about proper storage and handling. I began supplying them with Stanadyne Performance Formula additive to compensate for the loss of lubricity inherent in low sulfur fuels. I also showed them how to judge where the pump-to-engine timing should be after an injection pump was timed to the engine with timing marks (see Fig. 4-6, p. 62).

With small investment and effort, this towing company reaped the benefits of greater reliability and longer life of their diesel engines.

I was happy to have helped this customer avoid further unnecessary expense. We were now supplying them with water separators, fuel filters, and fuel additive. When a fuel injection unit needed repair or replacement, the owner was more than happy to pay the slightly higher price our shop charged for a complete, quality fuel system service, and he has been a loyal customer ever since. How much money could this towing company have saved if they'd had this handbook from the beginning? I hope others can avoid the grief and extra expense caused by the lack of basic information.

Making the effort to properly maintain your engine and fuel injection system should be part of a greater effort to provide complete maintenance for all other equipment systems. Coolants, gear oils, transmission fluids, grease, etc., should be maintained and changed according to the manufacturer's requirements. Proper maintenance will extend the life of your engine and equipment and save you money.

Choosing a mechanic

Choosing a competent mechanic or repair shop is essential. We've all heard the horror stories of the mechanics or repair shops that didn't have the proper tools, equipment, training, information, etc., who performed unnecessary repairs or who made a bad problem worse. In the end, these poorly trained mechanics only cost you time and money.

When looking for a mechanic or a repair shop, consider some of the following criteria: Has the mechanic or shop been in business for a long time in the same area? Are the mechanics trained and certified? Is the shop an Original Equipment Manufacturer (OEM) dealer for your vehicle or equipment? Even though the shop labor rate may be higher than a non-dealer shop, if you take your equipment to an OEM dealer, the technicians are usually very well trained.

If you are unfamiliar with a mechanic or repair shop, it is not improper to ask for references. Ask other diesel owners about mechanics or repair shops in your area. When you decide on a mechanic or repair shop, you will have good knowledge from this handbook to verify whether any engine and/or fuel system repairs are necessary. For example, if your John Deere diesel tractor is making some white exhaust, is a little low on power, and your mechanic tells you the injectors need to be repaired or replaced, you will know that injectors are most likely not the cause of the problem.

Other related information is important for correct and complete diagnosis. Did the problem happen suddenly or gradually? Did the problem start shortly after fueling? Have other repairs been made or attempted recently? All these different pieces of information, whether related to the engine problem or not, must be considered in the diagnosis. The basic procedure for diagnosing and repairing an engine or fuel system problem is:

1) Identify the problem;
2) Identify the cause;
3) Test the cause if possible (sometimes testing the cause means replacing the part that you suspect is bad);
4) Fix it.

With the very high cost of parts and labor, it is important that a complete diagnosis is made. Be aware of any warranties applying to your equipment or engine. Specific procedures need to be followed to qualify for a warranty repair.

If an engine problem has been diagnosed and a fuel system component has been identified as causing the problem, take a few things into consideration. Find out the expected life of the unit from your local diesel fuel injection shop. If your unit has run less than half of its expected life, a test may be a proper course of action. If a pump or injector has had good filtered fuel and no water has run through it, a bench test may be in order. An injector from an injection pump/injection line/injector system can be tested easily by a fuel injection shop. Many shops perform injector tests at little or no charge. An injection pump test, however, can take from one to three hours depending on the pump manufacturer and pump model.

Choose a fuel injection shop that is authorized by the manufacturer of your fuel injection system. Many maverick (non-authorized) pump shops exist but they will not have current training, equipment, or information. They will also be unable to provide manufacturer's warranty service. Although some maverick shops do good work, they are handicapped by a lack of current factory information and training.

If a complete component repair or replacement is needed, you will be satisfied that the problem has been correctly identified and that all other possibilities have been eliminated. With the theory presented in this handbook, and with proper diagnosis, an engine or fuel system problem can be identified and corrected with the smallest amount of time and money.

Although new and remanufactured fuel injection components are available from vehicle or equipment dealers, the best quality and prices for fuel injection repairs and exchange units can generally be found at authorized fuel injection shops. Like any repair business, quality and prices will vary from one fuel injection shop to another.

Chapter 10 - The Future of Diesel

With emissions requirements becoming more and more stringent, diesel engines and fuel injection systems are constantly being improved. Injection pressures are becoming higher to make finer atomization and to decrease duration of injection. Injection timing and fuel system governing are becoming more precise by means of electronics. Some engine manufacturers are developing devices to change the timing of engine valves for optimum air intake and exhaust characteristics. Injecting platinum vapor or urea vapor into the exhaust stream is a promising new technology for reducing NOx. Fuel refineries are being required to produce lower sulfur fuels to reduce pollution. Even biodiesel made from soybeans and which contains no sulfur is breaking into the diesel fuel market.

With all the improvements and refinements, the newest diesel engines all have one thing in common -- they are still diesels. They must be properly maintained and supplied with good quality fuel that has been properly filtered and free of water. The engine compresses air to make heat and the fuel injection system must pressurize, time, and meter the fuel. The injector or nozzle must atomize and distribute the fuel in the cylinder. Timing devices will adjust start-of-injection timing as needed so that the maximum cylinder pressure from expansion and combustion occurs just after TDC. The operator or fuel system governor regulates fuel metering for any working moment.

Any diesel engine or fuel system problem will have specific symptoms with colored exhaust or no visible exhaust. The exhaust is usually the key to understanding, diagnosing, and correcting an engine or fuel system problem.

A diesel engine equipped with an electronic governor as opposed to a mechanical governor is not a scary thing. It will still govern starting fuel, idle, midrange, full load, high idle, and governor cutoff. As before, the operator will have an accelerator or throttle device to control part-load conditions. The difference is in the precision of the governing.

Higher injection pressures, tighter timing requirements, improved engine designs, lower sulfur fuels, and electronic governing make up the future for the diesel engine. You can be sure that any currently manufactured diesel engine will run clean under any normal working conditions.

Although engines and fuel systems will continue to improve, the future for diesel is now. Electronic governing was introduced in the early 1990s and has progressed dramatically.

The ultimate fuel injection system in today's diesel engine is the electronically controlled unit injector. These units function mostly like a Detroit injector with a cam working on the injector to control pressurization and timing. The 25,000 psi and higher injection pressures needed for emission requirements are achieved with this design. Instead of a mechanical rack changing the fuel metering, an electronic servo does the job. An onboard computer that receives data from various sensors controls governing and start-of-injection timing for the engine. Depending on engine RPM, throttle position, engine load, turbocharger boost, and any number of other conditions, the governor program sends a signal to the servo unit of the injector so that the injector will deliver properly metered fuel at the right time for any working moment. The electronically governed unit injector is the simplest yet most precise diesel fuel injection system currently being produced.

A unique unit injector system, the hydraulic electronic unit injector (HEUI), has been incorporated into Ford trucks with a Navistar Powerstroke 7.3-liter turbocharged engine.

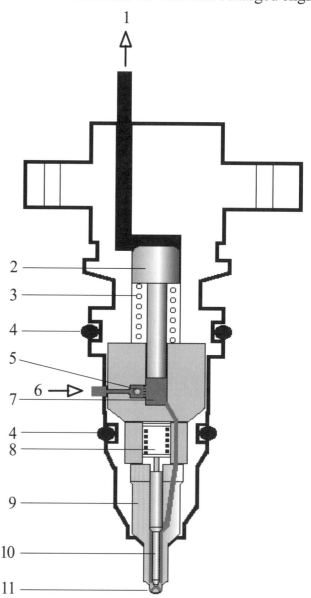

Fig. 10-1. HEUI during charging cycle.

1 High-pressure oil supply
2 Intensifier piston
3 Intensifier piston spring
4 Fuel gallery o-ring
5 Check ball
6 Pressurized fuel supply
7 Pumping chamber
8 Spring cage
9 Nozzle assembly
10 Needle valve
11 Nozzle spray hole

The pumping chamber is charged from a fuel gallery in the engine cylinder heads. The fuel gallery is supplied with filtered and water-separated fuel from a supply pump. During the charging cycle, the intensifier piston has moved up to allow fuel to enter the pumping chamber.

The HEUI, designed by Caterpillar, uses precisely regulated high-pressure oil movement to control pressurization, timing, and metering of the diesel fuel. Instead of a camshaft moving the pumping unit to create injection pressure, engine oil is used with a separate oil pumping system to create the force needed for injection. The oil pressure is increased incrementally to a maximum pressure of about 4000 psi. The intensifier piston creates a maximum injection pressure of 30,000 psi.

Pressurization and timing of injection is controlled by high-pressure oil pulsations which force the intensifier piston down and compress fuel in the pumping chamber. The injection pressure created lifts the needle valve off its seat and forces fuel through the nozzle spray holes. The fuel is atomized and distributed into the cylinder's hot compressed air.

Fuel metering is also controlled by the high-pressure oil pulsations. Between injections, a certain volume of oil is retracted, which controls the upward movement of the intensifier piston. If a larger amount of oil is retracted between injections, the intensifier piston moves fully upward, which maximizes the fuel volume in the pumping chamber. If a smaller volume of oil is retracted between injections, the intensifier piston moves upward, but not fully. The amount of oil retracted between injections controls the fuel volume available for the pumping chamber, thus controlling the amount of fuel delivered during the next injection cycle.

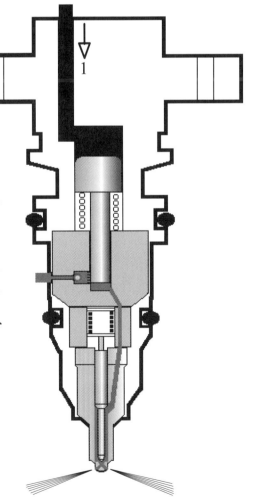

Fig. 10-2. HEUI during injection cycle.

Each injector is supplied with oil pressure between 450 psi and 4000 psi through a common rail. A solenoid and poppet valve on top of each injector (not shown), slaved by an electronic control module (ECM), admits and retracts oil pressure to/from the top of the intensifier piston. The vehicle's onboard computer system controls the injector solenoid and poppet valve to admit and retract oil pressure as needed. Pressurization, timing, metering, and even duration of injection have become part of a computer program.

The HEUI system is revolutionary, but even with this most advanced fuel injection system, the engine is still a diesel. The engine must compress air and create heat. The fuel injection system must pressurize, time, and meter the fuel while the injector or nozzle atomizes and distributes the fuel into the engine cylinder's hot compressed air. Retarded timing, low compression, or a cold engine will cause white exhaust. Poor atomization, advanced timing, insufficient oxygen, or overfueling will cause black exhaust. Fuel supply restrictions will cause a loss of power. Air ingress problems will cause the engine to run rough constantly or intermittently, lose power, surge, run and stall, and be difficult to restart or not start at all. Any fuel injection system must be supplied with perfectly clean, water-free, good quality diesel fuel. The model of a diesel engine along with its various problems and associated symptoms that I have set forth in this handbook will apply well into the future.

Diesel technology will continue to improve and manufacturers will continue to strive to produce cleaner and more efficient engines. But whether your diesel was made in the 1940s, in the 1990s, or later, and whether your engine is in a car, truck, tractor, boat, generator, or other industrial equipment, it is still a diesel. When problems arise, always remember to look at the exhaust and use the guidelines for troubleshooting set forth in this handbook. I strongly recommend reading this handbook again and keeping it available for reference.

Proper maintenance and a little extra care will pay off down the road as you get the most reliability and extend the life of your diesel engine.

Troubleshooting Charts

The following troubleshooting charts consolidate all the troubleshooting information discussed throughout the handbook. These charts are not meant to replace engine service manuals but to aid you in identifying problems, symptoms, and possible causes of a malfunctioning diesel engine.

The troubleshooting charts list diesel engine problems, system variations, associated exhaust, possible causes, pertinent notes, and page numbers where the problems are discussed in the handbook. Unless otherwise noted, all engine problems are for a warmed-up engine using suitable fuel. White exhaust can mean white exhaust with a bluish tint.

Problem	Variation	Exhaust	Possible Causes	Notes	Page(s)
Loss of power	All	Clean	Throttle arm not hitting high-speed screw	Engine will not reach full RPM	48
			Shut-off lever not fully open		48
			Fuel supply restriction or tank cap not venting	May cause white exhaust	48, 69, 72, 73, 76
			Air in fuel supply	Engine may run rough and/or surge. May cause white exhaust	48, 71, 73, 76, 80
			On/off solenoid malfunction or insufficient voltage		48
	Stanadyne or Lucas-CAV distributor pump	Clean	Return line restriction	May cause white exhaust	48, 49, 54, 69, 70
	Inline injection pump	Clean	Overflow valve failure	May cause white exhaust	74
	Pump/line/injector	Clean	Defective injection pump		49
	Turbocharged engine w/ aneroid	Clean	Boost pressure leak Turbocharger or wastegate failure Aneroid failure		89

Problem	Variation	Exhaust	Possible Causes	Notes	Page(s)
Light to moderate white exhaust, normal power	All	White	Cold weather		49, 50
			Poor quality fuel		65
			Defective thermostat	Engine runs cold	54
			Defective injector	Rough running and/or engine miss associated	53, 54, 81
			Full or partial timing device failure		51, 54
			Small loss of compression	Greater loss of compression increases white exhaust and power loss	3, 51, 52, 53, 55
			Blown head gasket, loss of coolant, one or more cylinders low on compression	Associated rough running and/or engine miss	50, 52, 53
	Stanadyne or Lucas-CAV distributor pump	White	Partial injection pump return line restriction	More severe restriction will cause loss of power	48, 54, 69, 70
	Distributor injection pump	White	Partial fuel supply restriction	More severe restriction will cause loss of power	48, 72, 73, 76

Problem	Variation	Exhaust	Possible Causes	Notes	Page(s)
Light to moderate white exhaust, normal power	Pump/line/injector	White	Starting aid not shutting off after start-up		83, 124
			Wear or breakage of injection pump drive components causing retarded start-of-injection timing	Engine runs cooler and quieter	50, 51
			Defective injection pump		54, 56
White exhaust at low idle	All	White	Cold engine		49, 54, 55
			Timing device failure		51, 54
			Low compression	Associated white exhaust during operation	3, 52, 53, 55
	Stanadyne or Lucas-CAV distributor pump	White	Partial fuel supply or return line restriction	Associated white exhaust and possible loss of power during operation	48, 54, 72, 73, 76
	Pump/line/injector	White	Retarded pump-to-engine timing		50, 51, 54
			Starting aid not shutting off after start-up		83

Problem	Variation	Exhaust	Possible Causes	Notes	Page(s)
Loss of power	All	White	Air in fuel supply		48, 71, 73, 76, 80
			Severely retarded injection timing	Engine runs cooler and quieter	51, 54, 55
			Fuel tank filled with gasoline or other unsuitable fuel	Symptoms begin shortly after fueling	56
			Poor quality fuel, fuel contamination causing injector needle valve to stick open, nozzle breaks apart		53, 65
			Significant loss of compression	Engine runs cooler and quieter	3, 55, 56
	Stanadyne or Lucas-CAV distributor pump	White	Return line restriction		48, 54, 69, 70
	All	Clean or white	Fuel supply restriction, supply pump failure, tank cap not venting		48, 56, 69, 72, 73, 76
	Inline injection pump	White	Overflow valve failure		74
	Pump/line/injector	White	Defective injection pump		56, 115

Problem	Variation	Exhaust	Possible Causes	Notes	Page(s)
Light to moderate black exhaust, normal power	All	Black	Small air restriction		57, 90
			Operating engine at higher altitudes		59
			Poor quality fuel		65
			Improper atomization, worn injectors		56, 57, 81
			Overfueling		57
			EGR system failure		60
			Small compression loss	Engine produces more white exhaust while warming up. More compression loss turns exhaust to gray and/or white	3, 52
	Pump/line/injector	Black	Advanced pump-to-engine timing, worn or misadjusted timing device	Engine runs hotter and louder	58, 59
	Turbocharged engine w/ aneroid	Black	Aneroid out of adjustment	Black exhaust on acceleration	90
	Turbocharged engine, no aneroid	Black	Boost pressure leak	Possible loss of power	90
	Turbocharged engine w/ charge-air cooler	Black	Charge-air cooler failure	Possible loss of power	90

Problem	Variation	Exhaust	Possible Causes	Notes	Page(s)
Moderate to heavy black exhaust, normal power	All	Black	Improper atomization, severely worn injectors		56, 57, 60
			EGR system failure		60
			Overfueling		57, 60
	Turbocharged engine w/ aneroid	Black	Aneroid failure, aneroid blocked, or aneroid out of adjustment	Black exhaust on acceleration	90
	Turbocharged engine, no aneroid	Black	No aneroid	Black exhaust on acceleration	90
Moderate to heavy black exhaust, low power, or engine won't run	All	Black	Complete or near complete air restriction or turbocharger failure		57, 60, 61, 90
			Overloaded engine		61
			Poor quality fuel		65
Loss of power, light to moderate black exhaust	All	Black	Combination problem of worn injectors, restricted air supply, severely advanced injection timing, and any possible cause listed in 'Loss of power, clean exhaust.'		56, 57, 61
			Poor quality fuel		65
Black and white exhaust	All	Black and white, or gray	Combination problem		63
	Pump/line/injector	Black and white, or gray	Crossed injection lines		63

Problem	Variation	Exhaust	Possible Causes	Notes	Page(s)
Blue exhaust	All	Blue	Severely worn engine	Beware of runaway engine	63
	Turbocharged engine	Blue	Turbocharger oil seal failure		91
			Air restriction		91
Brown exhaust	All	Brown	Dirty fuel from corroded fuel tank		63, 64
Pumping unit seizure	All		Water contamination, gasoline, or fuel viscosity too low		56, 65, 66, 126
	Stanadyne or Lucas-CAV distributor pump		Banjo bolt bottoming in hydraulic head. Sealing washers flattened or missing		127, 128
	Pump/line/injector		Plugged injector, plugged injection line, injector opening pressure too high		126
			Injection pump misalignment		126
			Water or other liquid sprayed on injection pump while engine is running		124, 125
Constant or intermittent rough running, surging, engine stalls	All	Clean or colored	Air in fuel supply		48, 71, 73, 76, 80, 81, 107
Combination problem	All	Clean or colored	Each problem must be identified and corrected		60, 61, 63, 82

Problem	Variation	Exhaust	Possible Causes	Notes	Page(s)
Hard starting or no starting	All	White	Engine not turning fast enough at cranking speed		79
		Clean	Solenoid malfunction, no voltage to solenoid, shut-off lever closed or not fully open		79
			Air in fuel supply		71, 73, 76, 79, 80, 107
		Colored	Fuel tank filled with gasoline	Loss of power	56
		Clean or white	Severe fuel supply restriction		69, 72, 73, 76, 79
			Pumping units beginning to wear	Engine runs normally after starting	82
			Fuel supply has bled back	Tank must be lower than injection pump	80-81
			Defective injector(s)		81
	Pump/line/injector	Clean or white	Defective injection pump		69, 79, 82
	Prechamber engine	White	Glow plug system failure		81, 82, 130
	All	White	Cold engine, retarded injection timing, starting aid failure, defective injectors, low compression		3, 81, 82, 83
	All	Black	Massive air restriction or excessive load		57, 83
			Worn injectors	Usually doesn't cause the problem but can contribute	56, 57, 83

Problem	Variation	Exhaust	Possible Causes	Notes	Page(s)
Engine stalls	All	White	Cold engine, retarded injection timing, fuel tank filled with gasoline, low compression		56, 84
		Clean or white	Idle RPM too low, fuel supply restriction, air in fuel supply, solenoid voltage supply interrupted, defective injection pump or fuel system governor		48, 71, 76, 80, 81, 84, 100, 107
	Stanadyne or Lucas-CAV distributor pump	Clean or white	Return line restriction		54, 84
Engine oil dilution	Injection pump driven or engine driven supply pump		Defective supply pump		118
	Injectors, injection lines and return lines under valve cover		Injection line or return line leakage		118-119
	Inline injection pump		Cracked barrel or defect in barrel sealing area	Caused by plugged injector or injection line. Associated rough running or engine miss	118-119
	Distributor injection pump		Drive shaft bearing or drive shaft seal failure	Pump drive exposed to crankcase	119

Index

return fuel (line), 11, 21, 31, 54, 56, 69, 70-77, 93, 102, 107, 108, 118
  restriction, 48, 49, 54, 69-70, 77, 84, 93, 124
rod, connecting. *See* connecting rod
rod, control. *See* control rod
roller tappet, 11, 14, 20
Roosa Master. *See* Stanadyne
RPM, 27
runability, 1
runaway engine, 63, 91

S

safety, 2
  safety concerns, 51, 53, 59, 61, 63, 82, 92, 100, 107, 124, 125, 126, 130
sealing washer, 127-128
seizure. *See* pumping unit seizure
sleeve metering, 108-114, 116
solenoid, 21, 48, 84, 107, 108, 131, 137
soot. *See* particulates
spark plug, 4-5, 53
stalling, 48, 54, 56, 71, 76, 80, 81, 84, 100, 107, 138
Stanadyne, 21, 27, 54, 93, 119-124
Stanadyne Performance Formula, 68, 69, 132
starting aid, 79, 81-83
starting fluid, 82
static timing. *See* timing, pump-to-engine
supercharger, 91
supply line, 70-72, 75, 76, 80, 102,
supply pump, 70, 72-77, 93, 99, 118
  pressure side, 72, 75, 80
  suction side, 72, 74, 75, 76, 77, 80, 107

T

tachometer, 84
tank cap. *See* fuel tank cap
TDC, 16
Thermostart, 83
thermostat, 54
throttle, 10, 21, 28-29, 43-44, 48, 49, 99, 106, 107, 108, 119, 120, 121, 135, 136
timing, 10-11, 14-18, 25-26, 32, 33, 36, 37, 39-42, 45, 50-51, 53, 54, 55, 56, 58, 59, 61, 62, 63, 64, 82, 99, 100, 101, 102, 106, 107, 112-113, 119, 120, 123-124, 132, 135, 137, 138
  advanced, 18, 40-42, 54, 58, 59, 60, 61, 62, 63, 64, 100, 106, 124, 138

pump-to-engine, 14, 15, 20, 25, 26, 51, 55, 58, 59, 61, 62, 82, 83, 112, 113, 119, 120, 124
  retarded, 18, 37, 40, 42, 50-51, 53-55, 56, 59, 61, 62, 63, 64, 84, 100, 124, 138
timing device(s), 18, 21, 26, 40-42, 45, 48, 51, 54-55, 59, 62, 106, 108, 113, 135
timing marks, 51, 61, 119, 120, 121, 122, 123
transfer pump. *See* supply pump
turbocharger, 63, 85-91, 93, 94, 98, 106, 131
turbo lag, 86-88, 90, 91, 106
two-stroke engine, 93-100

U

underfueling, 49, 89, 100, 107
underrun, 29, 84, 87
United Technologies. *See* Ambac

V

valve
  delivery. *See* delivery valve
  exhaust, 3, 4-7
  intake, 3, 4-7
  metering. *See* metering valve
  needle. *See* injector, needle valve
  nozzle. *See* injector, nozzle (valve)
  overflow. *See* overflow valve (screw)
vaporization, 36, 51, 56, 57, 60
viscosity, 65, 126

W

warranty, 48, 134
wastegate, 88, 89
water separation, 65, 66-67, 69, 70, 71, 72, 73, 80, 93, 100, 102, 107, 117, 126, 132, 138
white fuel vapor. *See* fuel vapor, white

Z

Zexel, 93

Notes

Please copy this page:

Title: Understand Your Diesel Engine and Save Money   **Author:** Robert L. Lekse
ISBN No. 0-9722695-0-9

To Order More Copies:

Telephone orders:
Call toll-free within the United States 24 hours a day: 800-247-6553.
Phone orders calling from outside the United States: 419-281-1802.
Please have your credit card ready.

Online orders: www.yourdiesel.com. Follow links to the ordering page.

Fax orders: Complete this form and fax to 419-281-6883. Credit card orders only.

Mail orders: Checks and money orders only.   **BookMasters, Inc.**
Checks are payable to BookMasters, Inc. Fill in   **P.O. Box 388**
the information below and mail this order form to: **Ashland OH 44805**

- -

Delivery by USPS Media Mail within the United States. Allow 1-4 weeks for delivery. For larger orders, special pricing, and rush delivery, please call 800-247-6553.

International orders: Please order online or call 419-281-1802.

Copies	Price	S&H
1	$20.00	$3.90
2	34.00	5.26
3	51.00	5.68
4	68.00	6.10

Title:	**Copies:**	**Price:**	**Total:**
Understand Your Diesel Engine and Save Money	_____	Use chart	_____

Ohio and Florida residents: Please add applicable sales tax   _____

Shipping and handling: Use chart   _____

Please pay this amount: $_____

Payment: Money Order ☐   Credit Card ☐   Check ☐
Credit Card: Visa ☐   MasterCard ☐   American Express ☐   Discover ☐

Credit Card Number:_____ Exp. Date ____/____

Name on card:_____

Mailing address:
Name:_____
Address: _____
City, State:_____ Zip _____
Daytime telephone:_____
E-mail address:_____

All personal information is kept confidential.